IT WAS GOOD I WAS AFFLICTED

Gail A Henry-Walker

If I could go back in time, I would tell myself

that everything will be okay.

LGT PUBLISHING HOUSE
UPCOMING 2015 BOOKS

BUSINESS
ZERO DOLLAR STARTUP

~

INSPIRATIONAL/SPIRITUAL
WALK WITH GOD DAILY DIARY
NOT MY TIME TO DIE

~

CHILDREN
DIMPLES & FRIENDS: PUT SAFETY 1ST SERIES
DIMPLES SHOUTS, "STRANGER DANGER"

OH NIYLAH!

KINDERGARTEN... OH BOY!

IT WAS GOOD I WAS AFFLICTED

Trials, Tests, Struggles, Transformation and Messages from God

GAIL A HENRY-WALKER

An Imprint of

My purpose in life is to help girls and women who have been battered physically, mentally and spiritually by people and life, achieve a greater sense of peace, clarity, and spiritual awareness.

⁓

It is my time to step into God's light, God's truth, and His purpose. I will stand boldly in God's truth naked and exposed, with openness and love.

~ Gail A Henry-Walker ~

Published by
LGT Publishing House
Greenbelt, MD 20770

Edited by
Matthew J. La Rocco
Cover Designed by
JESH ART STUDIO

Illustration by
ARDIANSYAH
Formatted by
LGT Publishing House

ISBN: 0692397779
ISBN-13: 978-0692397770
1st Edition, 2015
Published in the United States of America
Contact info: info@lgtpublishinghouse.com or lgtpublishinghouse@gmail.com
http://www.gailahenry.com http://lgtpublishinghouse.com

DEDICATION

This book is dedicated foremost to God my Father because of all the great things He has done in my life. I am and will forever be grateful that He called my name, tagged me in, saved me, delivered me, resurrected me and transformed me. To my son DeVaughn P.T Walker, Jr. who supports me in everything I do and for loving me unconditionally.

To the girls and women who have been used and abused by people and life, I want to let you know that you are a lot stronger than you know and the fact that you are still standing and fighting for survival proves it. Reach for Jesus and allow Him to take you through whatever trials, tests and struggles you may face and transform you and your life forever.

I Love You. -Blessings

CONTENTS

ACKNOWLEDGMENTS

To The Me I Had To Leave Behind

My Dear Old Me,

If I was to say that I will miss you, that would be a lie. You see, there comes a time in life when old things and ways have to come to an end and die for the new to take shape, grow and thrive. Although you have valiantly served your purpose dear friend, you still had to go.

You were no longer needed for me to survive because I asked God for His grace and now through the new me His light can shine. When I called out to Him, He answered the call. My life has been changed for the better but the old me (you) had to fall away.

Because of all the things you went through, God was able to reveal to me my true purpose and why you went through the things you did. My purpose is to help girls and women who have been battered physically, mentally, and spiritually by people and life achieve a greater sense of peace, clarity, and spiritual awareness. I will do this by telling our story in a detached and healthy positive way, which is my testimony of God's love, patience, grace and mercy. I will tell of our journey and ultimate transformation.

It is my time to step into God's light, God's truth, and His purpose for my life. I will stand boldly in God's truth about who I am, naked and exposed, with openness and love.

Goodbye Old Friend,

Gail A Henry-Walker

NOTE FROM THE AUTHOR

It has taken me 43 years to learn and know God's truth for me. That's a long time to search for one's purpose in life. Well, what I realized was that although it was great to finally reach the destination of knowing, it was the process that came before the understanding that was most important.

All my life lessons and how I lived through them is up for display. All the tools I developed to help create the necessary changes within myself is available to anyone who wishes to use them.

True and "Permanent Life Change" is achieved slowly but steadily. It cannot be rushed neither can it be ignored. Life is a perpetual state of change. There were times when my strength and will was tested. It became increasingly important that I avoided becoming too malleable. I had to stay strong.

Each time I fell, I got back up, dusted myself off and kept pressing forward. I have to admit that I was dizzy and a bit shaky when I got up, but I had to steady myself. There were also times in which I found myself in places I never knew existed. When those moments came, I held on tightly to my faith and God's promise. Because I persevered, what I received at the end of my journey was priceless and life changing.

Everything I once was, everything I am, and everything I will become is on display. I am exposed, naked and unafraid.

- Gail A Henry-Walker.

PSALM 119:71 KING JAMES VERSION (KJV)

[71] IT IS GOOD FOR ME THAT I HAVE BEEN AFFLICTED;
THAT I MIGHT LEARN THY STATUTES.

CHAPTER 1

IT WAS GOOD I WAS AFFLICTED

CHAPTER 1

IT WAS GOOD I WAS AFFLICTED

Psalm 119:71 King James Version (KJV) [71] It is good for me that I have been afflicted; that I might learn thy statutes.

I have gone through a great deal in my lifetime and for a very long time I was angry, bitter, unforgiving and in pain. I used to constantly ask God why I had to keep going through those things I had to endure but I was always met with silence. It may have taken me a while to figure it out but ... *Romans 8:28 King James Version (KJV) 28 And we know that all things work together for good to them that love God, to them who are the called according to his purpose.*

When you've been called and chosen to do something for God, life will often times than most serve you up some traumatic circumstances for you to go through. Many times you will find yourself in a pressing place. 2 Corinthians 4:8-10 King James Version (KJV) [8] *We are troubled on every side, yet not distressed; we are perplexed, but not in despair; 9 Persecuted, but not forsaken; cast down, but not destroyed; 10 Always bearing about in the body the dying of the Lord Jesus, that the life also of Jesus might be made manifest in our body.*

You are placed in pressing places because God is squeezing out of you that which is needed to manifest within you for God's plan to be revealed within and then birthed out of you. But, just know that it is always for the best even if it does not feel like it at that time. You will end up better for it.

All I can tell you is that each time I went down, I came up better than I was when I went down. I may have been wounded, but I healed and I am better for it. I may have wandered through the darkness, but I came through the other side better for it. I couldn't see where I was going many times, but it left me with no other choice but to grab hold of Jesus, so I came out better for it.

I may not have liked where I was and what I had to bear, but I came out better for it. God took me through a 10 year season of outer drought by fertilizing, watering and tending to my inner being, my spirit and my soul. While my outer life was in shambles, God rebuilt me on the inside. One by one He began to address and destroy strongholds, generational curses, spirits, untrue beliefs, addictions, pain, unforgiveness, brokenness, emptiness, idols and so much more.

I knew I was chosen because of the magnitude of the afflictions throughout my life. The devil has been trying to destroy me my entire life and he ensured I started off with maximum pain in an effort to hold me down. So you see I had to be afflicted. I may not have liked it, but since God allowed it to happen it wasn't without purpose.

When God broke down and destroyed the things within me that did not serve me or Him, I became the person I always hoped I could be. It's funny, for most of my life I never felt like I was loved and now I know that not only am I loved and always had been, but I AM THE GREATEST EXPRESSION OF GOD'S LOVE. God loved me into submission and acceptance. I never knew that was possible.

All I know is that if I had not been afflicted, I would never have known the full extent of God's Glory. This is why I say, "It Was Good I Was Afflicted."

THANK YOU FOR BEING MY GREATEST INSPIRATION AND
CHEERLEADER

CHAPTER 2

ATTITUDE OF GRATITUDE

CHAPTER 2

ATTITUDE OF GRATITUDE

Dear heavenly father, thank you for leading my steps along my journey to reaching my fullest potential and living my purpose. Thank you for transforming me into the person you need me to be, in order for me to do what you need me to do. Thank you for supplying me with unlimited positive energy that extends to everyone I encounter.

Thank you for providing me with an unlimited supply of abundance in all areas of my life. Thank you for using my desire to meet and know you to transform my life, my businesses, and every single person that comes into contact with me. Thank you for giving me the understanding that everything I do and every action I take must be for the betterment of others. Thank you for allowing my voice and your truth to be heard and allow it to penetrate into the core of everyone who hears, sees, and reads it.

Thank you for being my greatest inspiration and cheerleader. I will take what you have taught and revealed to me and pass it on to others. I pray that I will be an inspiration to those who hear and read my messages of transformation, hope, forgiveness, reconciliation, resurrection, faith, and healing. Father I ask that you allow my inner light to shine bright and long, so it reverberates throughout space and time and makes a great impact on all living beings.

I didn't always pray like that. This prayer was birthed out of pain, brokenness, trials, tribulations, and many lessons. It was God's transformation of me and my life that birthed this prayer and this level of gratitude out of me. The way I figure it... it was in seed form the whole time, I just didn't know it.

During my transformation, I learned that even though it was hard to maintain at times, it was imperative to develop a grateful heart, spirit and mind. I realized that no matter what was going on in my life I had to be grateful. When I wasn't being grateful my life became increasingly hectic. My mind would veer into negativity and my life would soon follow. Whatever you are holding firmly in your mind is what will show true in your life. Feeling and being grateful helps you to maintain a healthy positive balance.

I can still recall when my life was in complete and utter shambles. I could not believe what my life had become. When I was stuck in that place things felt and seemed dire. I felt like nothing was ever going to change and that my life was over. I was in a state of complete and utter darkness and I couldn't find anything to be grateful for. I was in a state of hopelessness in the midst of a thousand mile fog and I could not find my way out. The harder I fought to get out, the more entrenched in it I became.

During this time, I can honestly say that gratitude was not only a rarity, it wasn't even on my list of things to think about, much less feel. It was a concept that was really hard to grasp at that point in time. I would try to hold out hope but each time I did, something or someone would come along and dash any hope I was able to muster up.

The deeper I went into the fog the less grateful I became. I was only focusing on all the things that were wrong and those things I was lacking. I was in a very dark and dismal place. I tried everything to get out, to no avail. When I found myself completely out of options, I turned to the only Being I knew could help me.

When He came to my rescue, it was a great relief. He showed me that He was with me the whole time and I could have traveled through the fog and reached the other side a long time ago. The reason I had such a hard time was because I was trying to make it through all by myself. When you don't think you are deserving of anything good it is pretty hard to be hopeful for change much less being grateful.

When He rescued me, it was the first time that the word gratitude came to mind in a long time. He taught me how to be grateful again. Grateful is what I have been every day since, no matter what's happening in my life. I can't promise that it is easy, all I can say is that it is necessary. Without gratitude, your life will not look anything like what you think it should look like, want it to look like, or hope it will look like.

When I began my gratitude training I started small. Every day I made it a point to find small things to be grateful for. I know it may seem weird that I focused on the small things, but I learned early on not to take small things lightly. *Zechariah 4:10 For who hath despised the day of small things? for they shall rejoice, and shall see the plummet in the hand of Zerubbabel with those seven; they are the eyes of the LORD, which run to and fro through the whole earth.*

I started small so that I can strengthen my gratitude muscles. I had no idea that I had gratitude muscles but I did and it needed to be strengthened. Developing a grateful heart and mind required training and effort in order for me to strengthen my resolve to keep it up. It's just like any other muscle, if not used it becomes atrophied and must be rebuilt with nurturing and exercise.

I was knee deep in ungratefulness and it was time to curb that habit and establish an attitude of gratitude. It's not that there weren't many things to be grateful for, the biggest thing was waking up every morning, I just couldn't appreciate it. I was so entrenched in pain and out of practice, that I had to develop a system.

The first thing I did was make an agreement with myself that every day I needed to do a gratefulness check. I figured it would be easier if I found something to be grateful for first thing in the morning, starting with the fact that I woke up to see a new day. So my days started out with waking up and praying. As I prayed I would then tell God all the things I was thankful to Him for. Not only did the prayers bring peace to me it also helped to reinforce my training. I figured that my morning gratefulness check should be incorporated into something I already did (morning prayer, affirmations and meditation) to make it easier to remember to do it.

By doing this, I created an awesome habit that will continue throughout my life. The more I thought of things I was grateful for, the easier it was to build this new habit. It not only takes work to establish new systems, it also takes commitment. I was committed to myself. I was committed to change. I was committed to creating the right out-look for both my inner and outer world. I was committed to being in a perpetual state of gratefulness no matter what circumstances may come my way. Most of all, I was committed to increasing my faith, spiritual understanding; and my relationship with God.

I am glad I worked through my lack of gratitude because it has brought me closer to my Father than I ever thought was possible . I developed an Attitude of Gratitude and it has changed my outlook and my life.

I LOVE BEING THE PERSON GOD
HAS CALLED ME TO BE.

CHAPTER 3

WHO I AM AT MY CORE

CHAPTER 3

WHO I AM AT MY CORE

While power over others is the defense I once held closely, empowering others through positive willful actions and being an example of strength, kindness, unconditional love and determination is who I am at my core.

I choose to be my core self.

I choose empowerment versus power.

I choose peace over might.

I choose strength over tyranny.

I choose love over hate.

God has shown me how to use the greatest gift He could give a human being. It is unwavering and at times unfathomable. He gave me the gift of giving others "UNCONDITIONAL LOVE".

I love being the person God has called me to be.

IT WAS MY "COME TO JESUS MOMENT".

CHAPTER 4

HOW I ADDRESSED
MY NEGATIVE BEHAVIORS

CHAPTER 4

HOW I ADDRESSED MY NEGA-TIVE BEHAVIORS

This process was very difficult for me because it required me to look deep within myself and see the truth about myself. It was my «Come to Jesus Moment». I asked myself one simple question, but a difficult one to answer. What is it about myself that I do not like and requires immediate change? The answer(s) are not so easy to come by, because no one wants to admit to themselves that they are flawed and need work.

However, I knew I was flawed and needed work because if I wasn't, I would not be so unhappy and discontent. This was a process that began for me long ago. I was going through a very painful time in my life but even with the pain I wanted to get better. I wanted to get to the better me. I had already asked God to do a mighty work on me, but I also knew I needed to take responsibility for myself and change things within myself for me as well.

A great work was taking place and I needed to become fully engaged in the process. So, I went to work. I delved deep within my recesses and what I found astounded me. When I created the list of all the things I felt were negative, I had to sit there for a minute when I saw how many things were on my list. Don't laugh at me, but I came up with One Hundred and Nine things I wanted and needed to address about myself. They were weaknesses which were results of past pains that I had never dealt with or acknowledged but things I needed to overcome.

You read right, ONE HUNDRED AND NINE! What the .. do you know how painful that revelation was for me? It was at this moment that I said to myself, "What were you thinking doing this crap?" I was so mad at myself for coming up with what I thought was the greatest idea I had in a long time. That was because it turned into what I now viewed as the stupidest idea I ever had. I didn't feel better, I felt worse!

But ... yes there's always a "BUT"! I said the same thing to myself that I say to others, "Don't ask questions you don't really want to know the answer to."

I had no other choice, I had to begin the task of turning those negative behaviors into powerful positive behaviors. Yep, One Hundred and Nine! Here is what the end result of that was. I call it, my Negative Behavior Reprogramming Plan/Overcoming my Weaknesses. It took up six full pages. Six I tell yah!

I took the things that were negative and flipped them into positives. I typed it up and posted copies of the six sheets everywhere in my home. I posted them on my bathroom wall, bedroom wall, and living room wall. I did it so that everywhere I went I had no choice but to recite it each time I passed them. It took time for it to settle into my consciousness. This is because even though I wanted to change, my sinful mind had a plan of its own. It fought me tooth and nail every step of the way. To this very day it still tries to rear its ugly head, but because I am aware, I replace the negative thought and action I was about to take with positive ones.

Trust me when I tell you negative behavior is a "pain in the behind" to get rid of. They are downright dastardly. Yes, I said dastardly, I'm different like that. The worst part of making permanent changes is the opposition you get to the changes. What made it more puzzling, is the fact that the opposition wasn't coming from other people. The opposition was actually coming from within myself. My own mind was fighting me. What in the world! My own mind didn't want what's best for me?

Nah, that's not really the truth, but it sure is going to feel that way to you when you embark on this journey. My mind was simply trying to maintain the status quo. When new behavior is being introduced a fight will surely ensue. That's because to the subconscious mind, the new information was acting like a plague.

Push through the resistance and opposition. Fight for your best self to triumph. In order to reach your best self, you will have to fight like you have never fought before. The way your subconscious sees it, you will have become the enemy from within. Keep fighting. Keep reciting your positive behavior statements. Keep fighting, keep fighting, keep fighting until your subconscious mind gives way and accepts the new programming. This will be a battle if well fought will reap countless rewards for you in the future.

I should note that no matter how much work you do to change your negative behaviors, they have a nasty way of sneaking up on you, if you hadn't really worked completely through them. I have no idea what your list will comprise of or if you are even going to make a list of your own. All I can tell you is if you don't acknowledge there is a problem, you will never fix it. You will continue to go through the same situations, around the same mountains and walking in circles over and over again until you deal with things.

If you do decide to do this you must first list out all your negative behaviors especially those that many people have brought to your attention but you chose to ignore. Once you have that list, turn them into positive behaviors. Use I must or I will.

This powerful exercise helped me become the wonderful person I am today. You might ask, "Who says I'm wonderful"? Well, ME of course!

IT SHOULD BE SAID THAT IN ORDER TO CHANGE NEGATIVE BEHAVIORS, WE MUST FIRST ACKNOWLEDGE THOSE BEHAVIORS IN ORDER TO FIX IT.

CHAPTER 5

IT'S ALL IN THE MIND

CHAPTER 5

IT'S ALL IN THE MIND

It should be said that to change negative behaviors we must first acknowledge those behaviors in order to fix them. Then you have to work the program that bests suit you to shatter those habits/behaviors and replace them with new, positive and sustainable behaviors. I took my negatives and turned them into positive mantras. Here are some of the things I came up with.

1. I must be mindful of my tendency to be overly possessive of the people that I love and my possessions.
2. I must stabilize my life.
3. I must establish a regular routine.
4. I must get accustomed to making and keeping commitments.
5. I must remember that no one is self-sufficient all the time.
6. I must become active physically and socially.
7. I must communicate with tact.
8. I must not make promises I cannot or have no intentions on keeping.
9. I must strike a balance with giving of my material possessions and myself.
10. I must be aware of my tendency to be a hoarder.
11. I must remove the clutter from my life, environment, and my mind.
12. I must understand the difference between needs, wants, and desires.

13. I must implement consistency in my life, attitude, and how I do things.
14. I must become more decisive and less indecisive.
15. I must become less selfless.
16. I must learn and practice the art of patience.
17. I must learn how and when to say "NO".
18. I must remember that I do not need to seek other people's approval.
19. I must ask for what I want and need directly.
20. I must know my worth.
21. I must invest sufficient energy and time analyzing and making plans to realize my goals and dreams.
22. I must be gentle with my emotional needs and those around me.
23. I must place greater emphasis on moderation and self-discipline.
24. I must start practicing discriminate giving.
25. I must encourage the weak to become strong.
26. I must release my take no prisoner drive for power and social influence.
27. I must remember that the grass is not greener on the other side.
28. I must learn to channel my enthusiasm and vision in a non -hostile positive manner.
29. I must not allow others to take advantage of my kindness.
30. I must use my gifts to better the world and not just myself.
31. I must refrain from playing the part of the Martyr.
32. I must refrain from being an enabler.
33. I must stop avoiding open conflict.
34. I must stop avoiding or tuning-out problems because they cannot fix themselves.

35. I must develop a positive fighting spirit so I can overcome all obstacles.
36. I must turn my passiveness into my drive.
37. I must become my greatest cheerleader, fan and motivator.
38. I must eliminate all forms of laziness and negligence.
39. I must avoid my tendency of detaching myself from my immediate environment.
40. I must not wallow in self pity.
41. I must take strong, decisive, and definite action to change my life for the better.
42. I must organize my environment and remove any sign of chaos or clutter.
43. I must seek out positive outlets for my residual energy.
44. I must avoid allowing my spiritual values to color and cloud my perspective and approach to life in order to be a more open and understanding person.
45. I must calm my idealism and become more practical.
46. I must overcome my tendency of becoming high-strung and overzealous in pursuit of my endeavors.
47. I must learn how to relax and slow down.
48. I must recognize beforehand my tendency to overstep myself.
49. I must adopt a playful attitude to my life and their many challenges.
50. I must avoid trying to fix other people's lives.
51. I must avoid trying to fix other people.
52. I must obtain a poker face. (still terrible at this one)
53. I must stop trying to carry the world on my shoulders.
54. I must remember that no man is an island.
55. I must always let people know how much I care for them.
56. I must learn to relax, enjoy myself, and play sometimes.

57. I must stop taking life so seriously.
58. I must avoid the tendency to let my emotions overpower my reasoning and logic.
59. I must avoid my tendency of seeing things through rose-colored glasses.
60. I must overcome my tendency of being impulsive.
61. I must stabilize my life and get down to living.
62. I must remain persistent, especially in the face of adversity.
63. I must stand up for myself.
64. I must develop deeper intimacy and emotional bonds with people.
65. I must stick with the tried and true when it comes to relationship issues.
66. I must eradicate all traces of my violent and jealous tendencies.
67. I must be observant of my tendency to be self-indulgent and extravagant.
68. I must stop fighting against life's limitations and find solutions around them.
69. I must eradicate all tendencies of compulsive habits, behavior, desires, wants, and needs.
70. I must watch my tendency to be impatient.
71. I must learn the fine art of patience.
72. I must direct my competitive attitude to give rise to the common good of everyone, not just myself.
73. I must not separate myself from society because I need them and they need me.
74. I must remove my fear of rejection and failure. There is nothing wrong with failing and rejection will only make me stronger. Turn fears into positive drives.
75. I must become keenly aware of how my inner compulsions drive me.

76. I must stop, think, analyze, and evaluate before speaking or acting.
77. I must acknowledge when my stance is wrong and adjust it.
78. I must learn to take criticism better by hearing it, processing it, and letting go of the negative attributes.
79. I must stop taking other people's negative behaviors and attitude as a slight against me. I shall simply find the humor in it and let it go.
80. I must never sacrifice my happiness for others.
81. I must remember that martyrdom is pointless and senseless, but is unavoidable at times.
82. I must direct my strong sense of duty on behalf of myself.
83. I must use my drive for power and influence in the world for the good and betterment of all.
84. I must watch my tendency to display dogmatic and overzealous attitudes.
85. I must be mindful of overvaluing or undervaluing my possessions, assets, or self worth.
86. I must avoid extreme behavior in my personal and professional life.
87. I must remember to enjoy the fruits of my labor.
88. I must watch for any miserly tendencies.
89. I must appreciate what I have and not sweat about the things I do not.
90. I must let my hair down and enjoy as well as participate in spontaneous play and plain ole' fun.
91. I must forego all inclinations of other people's impression of me. The only impression that matters is mine. Am I being true to myself?
92. I must focus my competitive drive on improving my own record and myself.

93. I must focus on working to excel at something to make myself proud ... not others.

94. I must always remember that I am special and outstanding and I do not need to seek outside recognition for my efforts. I only need to seek it for myself.

95. I must remember that when I am under stress, not to focus on myself. Instead, focus on how things are going to affect the people around me.

96. I must strike a balance between doing for others and doing for myself.

97. I must understand my own tendency of dealing with money.

98. I must understand my own tendency of how I make a living.

99. I must understand my own tendency of how I build assets.

100. I must understand my own tendency of how I secure material bases.

101. I must understand my own tendency of using the resources I have.

102. I must remember that my world is little, but the outside world is expansive.

103. I must avoid any entanglements and involvement in other people's money matters, legal business, and personal affairs.

104. I must learn to become objective by not allowing my experiences or views to cloud my judgment.

105. I must at all cost avoid being dogmatic if my aim is to make a positive difference in people's lives and attitudes.

106 I must avoid displaying arrogant and assertive behaviors when dealing with people.

107. I must remember that I do not know everything and I must always be willing to learn.

108. The others are for my eyes only.

Why don't you try it out for yourself? Once you have that list, turn them into positive behaviors. Don't forget to use I must or I will.

It's important to post them throughout your environment so you can see and recite them numerous times daily on a consistent basis. If you can't see them, you won't recite them and if you don't recite them, you can't speak them over and into yourself. At first it may sound and seem like a lie but it won't be for much longer. Think it and you will become it.

I USED THESE "I WILL" AFFIRMATIONS ALONGSIDE OF
THE NEGATIVE BEHAVIOR REPROGRAMMING PLAN/
OVERCOMING MY WEAKNESSES.

CHAPTER 6

I WILL AFFIRMATIONS

CHAPTER 6

I WILL AFFIRMATIONS

I used these "I Will" affirmations alongside of the Negative Behavior Reprogramming Plan/Overcoming My Weaknesses affirmations. They added another layer to the process of getting my subconscious mind to accept my new life story. Every day for an entire year, I recited all the affirmations I created for myself. I did this every time I passed by them around my home.

There may be some that would ask me why? My response to that question would be, why not? The way I saw it, what did I have to lose? Absolutely nothing. I was retraining my brain to think and see life differently. I was going to do it for as long as I felt it necessary. It took years for me to develop all my thought habits so I was going to put in the time to reprogram my thought processes which in turn changed how I acted and responded to life and people.

1. I will apply CMA practices at all times and ensure I cross all T's and dot all I's.
2. I will be mindful of other people's needs and intentions.
3. I will think before I speak so my words don't get misconstrued.
4. I will be the best **ME** I can be for myself.
5. I will not allow people to take advantage of me or use me.
6. I will not overstep myself, regardless of the purpose or my intent.
7. I will give people the same level of respect that I expect from them, even if they do not give it in return. It's more important to me to remain true to myself.

8. I will keep an even keel at all times.
9. I will keep looking ahead to keep my eyes on my goals, while turning around at times to remember lessons learned.
10. I will remember that although my straight to the point personality serves me well, there are those that may be offended by it. It's more important not to alienate anyone.
11. I will remain detached from situations to allow myself to see the whole picture, not just what's in front of me.
12. I will remember that everyone won't like me and I can't please everyone and that's okay.
13. I will remind myself everyday that I am somebody, I do deserve respect, I do have a good heart, I do give 150% of myself/time/ love and I do deserve all the blessings that God has provided, is providing, and will continue to bestow upon me.
14. I will remind myself daily that there are many mind/guessing/ cat & mouse games being played by people, and a little straight-forward communication will make a huge positive difference.
15. I will show others more of my softer side so they know that I too am human.
16. I will show patience with others. Especially when they are difficult and unyielding, that is when I will show even more patience.
17. I will tell myself I love myself at least ten times a day.
18. I will be mindful of my stance, in an effort to ensure I am not perceived as hostile.
19. I will try to soften my words and personality as much as possible.
20. I will show love to others, especially when it may seem that there is no redeeming value in them… chances are they need it more than others and there "IS" redeeming value in everyone.
21. I will keep an open mind when others are sharing their view-point.

22. I will maintain the attitude of a student. There is always something to learn.
23. I will maintain an air of humility, never forgetting where I came from, what I have been through and the things I have done.
24. I will use my gifts to help as many people as I can during my lifetime.
25. I will follow my inner guidance system at all times. It is never wrong.
26. I will love hard, play hard and work smart.
27. I will remain open to trying new things.
28. I will spend more time listening and observing than speaking.
29. I will tell the people I love, that I love them often. It is important to me that they know how I feel about them.
30. I will not allow fear to prohibit me from taking risks.
31. I will not allow fear to prevent me from stepping outside of my comfort zone.
32. I will not allow fear to block me from accepting new opportunities.
33. I will not allow fear to stop me from showing people the real me.
34. I will no longer allow fear to make me dim my light.
35. I will forgive faster, so that I can let go of hurts quicker.
36. I will no longer allow hurts to fester within me and contaminate my body, mind, spirit and soul.
37. I will smile more, laugh harder and worry less.
38. I will love myself first and more.
39. I will focus less on myself and more on being of service to others.
40. I will become increasingly better at being patient.

IT WAS IMPORTANT THAT WHILE ON MY JOURNEY OF SELF
DISCOVERY AND TRANSFORMATION, I DID NOT NEGLECT
THE THINGS THAT ARE RIGHT AND POSITIVE ABOUT ME.

CHAPTER 7

WHAT YOU THINK
ABOUT YOURSELF MATTERS

CHAPTER 7

WHAT YOU THINK
ABOUT YOURSELF MATTERS

It was important that while on my journey of self discovery and transformation, I did not neglect the things that are right and positive about me. Just because I wanted to change negative attributes and behaviors, didn't mean the positive ones should go unnoticed.

I made a list of some of my positive attributes and posted them up alongside my negative reprogramming plan and affirmations, so that my subconscious mind didn't go into freefall. It's important that while I'm in such a delicate state of mind, I didn't just focus on what's wrong. Positive things about me needed to be addressed as well, because it is more of those attributes I wanted to replace the negative ones with.

Everyday I spoke these words over myself. I did not allow one day to go by without them passing through my lips. I have to be honest, there were times when I doubted if any of the things I was doing would work. I didn't have anyone that I knew who tested any of it. Although it would have been great to have someone to mentor me, I had the best mentor I could have ever asked for, God. Each day He strengthened my resolve to keep at it and not to give up. I was working towards giving rise to my best self so I had to keep at it. These are some of the words I spoke over and into myself each and every day for over a year.

1.   I love myself and each day I love myself even more.
2.   I love to set goals for myself.
3.   I achieve all goals I set, through my strong determination.

4. I take risks to break new ground.
5. I have great faith in God and bounce back quickly from disappointment and failure.
6. I am friendly and outgoing.
7. I have a great sense of fun and playfulness.
8. I have a philosophical mind.
9. I find workarounds when I hit obstacles or challenges.
10. I am very generous.
11. I dream big.
12. I am able to perceive the big picture, general patterns, and principles in things.
13. I am able to communicate different ways of looking at a situation that opens up new potential.
14. I believe in miracles and grace.
15. I never give up on life and inspire and encourage others to keep pushing forward.
16. I have a lovable and interesting demeanor.
17. I have a gentle laid back nature.
18. I am very gentle, sensitive, and receptive.
19. My intuition is unusually strong.
20. I am full of faith, spiritual, artistic, musically inclined, emotional, and imaginative.
21. I have great sensitivity and empathy for others.
22. I sense things physically and intuitively that proves to be correct.
23. I am tolerant and forgiving.
24. I am non-judgmental and accepting of people unconditionally, regardless of their flaws, mistakes or outward appearance.
25. I have a deep compassion for the suffering of all creatures and feel their pain as if it were my own.

26. I have great sympathy for the needy, disadvantaged, and misfits of society.
27. I express myself very well through writing, teaching, sharing ideas, and sharing information.
28. I am persuasive and fluent with the English language.
29. I have an introspective mind.
30. I am studious and somewhat of a bookworm when it comes to subject matters that interest me.
31. I am serious about my ambitions.
32. I am disciplined, dedicated, and tenacious in pursuit of my objectives.
33. I am hardworking and capable of forgoing immediate comfort in order to achieve my long-term goals.
34. I am realistic, pragmatic, and optimistic all at the same time.
35. I am always able to find a lesson in every situation.
36. I am an excellent strategist.
37. I attain success by formulating a conservative and workable plan and following through with it.
38. I have a high degree of sensitivity and compassion.
39. I have the ability to see the whole rather than only parts which comprise it.
40. I have an unusually expansive and far reaching outlook on life.
41. I am a very hard worker.
42. I am very intelligent.
43. I have an unconditional love for people that surpasses all understanding.
44. I am a loyal friend.
45. I am a wonderful mother.
46. I have a spirit that won't quit.

47. When I fail, I always get back up, dust myself off and keep moving forward by trying again.
48. I never quit and never say die.
49. I maintain a state of gratitude regardless of what present life looks like.

These are just a few of mine. Go ahead and create your own list. Don't leave anything out. Remember you have decided to take an active part in changing yourself and life for the better. You are now choosing to take your rightful place as a co-creator. Who and what will the new and best version of yourself be like? You are not in this alone, God, Jesus and your angels are there to help and strengthen you every step of the way.

You cannot gain true and permanent life changes without God the Father, God the Son and God the Holy Ghost. No matter what any non -believer says. It matters even if you used to or still think contrary to my statement. God and God alone can create the permanent changes within you that you seek. What I have learned, is that it is our lack of understanding and realization of this that causes us to wallow in self dependence, self pity, confusion, scarcity, self loathing, stagnation, negativity, and other self and life defeating habits for far too long.

Let God do what He does best. Let Him do all the heavy lifting. Our only job is to participate in the process and not impede Him and His work in us. Our job is to cry out to Him and allow Him to come into our life and become the BOSS. Whatever He says to do, do it. Wherever He says to go, go. Find and/or create tools for yourself to help yourself gain a better understanding of yourself and give yourself the ability to pay attention to the process. This is important. The process is vital. Pay more attention to the process than the destination.

All the work you are putting into yourself will be well worth it in the end. You can find time to put energy into work, family and other things that still leave you empty, lost, and depleted. It's time to put into yourself and God and allow Him, the process and your work within yourself to bring you to your best self. You deserve to become your best self.

WAKE EARLY TO PREPARE FOR EACH NEW DAY.

CHAPTER 8

SPEAK INTO EXISTENCE THE LIFE YOU WANT & WHO YOU WANT TO BECOME

CHAPTER 8

SPEAK INTO EXISTENCE THE LIFE YOU WANT & WHO YOU WANT TO BECOME

I recite these affirmations in addition to the scriptures daily. I wake early to prepare myself before I tackle each new day. I already know what my present life and situation is, my focus and affirmations is what I am speaking into and over myself and my future. I hope you find at least one affirmation that resonates with you.

1. All my dreams are coming to pass.
2. Everything about me is getting better and better.
3. Everything I do is supported and encouraged by my spirit and it never stops cheering me on.
4. God has broken down the walls that have kept me inside and away from my destiny and now I am free.
5. God has broken me free of all barriers that have kept me from becoming all that He has created me to be.
6. God has changed my life forever. He has provided me with breakthroughs, deliverance and transformations.
7. God has given me breakthroughs in areas of my life where I was once stagnant. Now there is movement in the right direction, never to go backwards.
8. God has made my enemies my footstool.
9. God has given me beauty for my ashes.
10. God has strengthened me and has renewed my life.

11. God has supplied all my needs according to His riches in Glory.
12. God used His key to unlock all areas of my life that prevented me from being whole and free, and I became whole and free.
13. God is about to show me something that I have never seen and It's going to be bigger, better and greater than I have ever imagined.
14. God is pleased with me.
15. I always know that I am in the perfect place because I know that God would never put me in the wrong place.
16. I am a child of the most high God.
17. I am beautiful both inside and outside.
18. I am blessed because my God has made an end to people and circumstances in my life that didn't serve me and replaced them with new beginnings and favor.
19. I am Blessed, Healthy, Strong, Wise and Youthful.
20. I am calm and peaceful.
21. I am forgiving of the mistakes of my past and towards others.
22. I am confident.
23. I am debt free.
24. I am disciplined.
25. I am focused.
26. I am forgiven.
27. I love to give of myself.
28. I am great at managing and manifesting positive things and circumstances in my life.
29. I am great in strength, confidence and endurance.
30. I am healthy.
31. I am highly favored.
32. I am in shape and I weigh what I should weigh.
33. I am love.

34. I am one of a kind.
35. I am prosperous.
36. I am redeemed.
37. I am secure.
38. I am slim, sexy, beautiful, and strong in body and mind.
39. I am strong in spirit.
40. I am talented.
41. I am the light of creation, pure and free.
42. Truth guides me in every step of my journey.
43. I am totally present in my body.
44. I am valuable and valued.
45. I am able to create ripples in the world to strengthen Gods Kingdom.
46. I am wearing a crown of favor.
47. I am well liked.
48. I can be extremely open and vulnerable with the people I love and trust.
49. I can do all things through Christ who strengthens me.
50. I create my life with my words, by expressing my desires, goals, and intentions openly with intense passion.
51. I easily set boundaries with others.
52. I experience my own need for love powerfully and openly ask for them to be met by those in my life.
53. I feel divinely guided, protected and safe.
54. I feel safe more than I feel anxious.
55. I find that I easily reach out to others to give and receive love.
56. I give of my wealth, time and talents to glorify God's kingdom and plans.
57. I have an awesome personality that has a hint of childlikeness.

58. I have been delivered from bad habits, negative thought patterns, and negative and untrue life stories.
59. I have been redeemed by the Lord.
60. I have been transformed into a woman of success, a woman who is confident in her words and actions. A woman who draws positive people and events into her life.
61. I have grace in the Lord and He has blessed me mightily.
62. I have Grace for this season.
63. I have more than enough.
64. I have Royal blood running through my veins.
65. I have unwavering faith and trust in God and feel connected to my soul and life purpose.
66. I hold only the highest and best thoughts for others in difficult moments (still a work in progress).
67. I forgive others easily and I am able to let go of painful feelings and experiences without malice.
68. I love being seen for who I really am.
69. I love how my body supports me.
70. I do not get or feel embarrassed about my emotions or needs.
71. I trust my instincts. It provides me with clarity and insight about my next steps.
72. I say God's truth even when it's hard.
73. I see myself as a reflection of God and that anything is possible in every moment, even if I can't or don't see it.
74. I see the big picture and how I fit in the world with my uniqueness and gifts.
75. I choose to see the world as infinitely abundant even in times of scarcity.
76. I am no longer afraid to allow my light to shine and show my brilliance, greatness, skills, value, desires, and faults.

77. I will never put my dreams aside again.
78. I will find unique ways to overcome obstacle as they appear in my life.
79. I release any and all energy within me that is not my own or of God.
80. It is my desire to allow God to use me however He wants to use me.
81. Love is something I give away freely and effortlessly.
82. Let my heart of love touch all who I encounter.
83. My dreams are becoming my reality.
84. My health, energy, and vitality consistently improve. I feel great!
85. My life is renewed and I will finish my course not abated and my eyes not dimmed.
86. My value comes from who I am, not what I do, or how much money I have.
87. New beginnings are in my future.
88. The rest of my life is filled with immeasurable blessings and the best moments of my life.
89. The right opportunities are headed my way.
90. The right people are in my future.
91. Things and life has shifted in my favor.
92. Those that are for me are greater in number than those that are against me.

FRIGHTENING, LIBERATING, EXCRUCIATINGLY PAINFUL,
MARVELOUS, AND BEAUTIFUL.

CHAPTER 9

I MET THE ME I ALWAYS WANTED TO BE

CHAPTER 9

I MET THE ME I ALWAYS WANTED TO BE

The work that was done on me internally by Jesus was awesomely executed and miraculous to experience. I will forever be grateful to God for everything that He has given me, He is doing for me, and for the things He has in store for me in the future. All I can tell you is that God had His work cut out for Him when it came to me. I had my work cut out for me. This undertaking was absolutely the most frightening, liberating, excruciatingly painful, marvelous, and beautiful experience I have gone through thus far.

I learned more about myself than I ever thought possible. I became the person I always wanted to be. It's like I woke up from a long slumber, or for a lack of a better term, I became unplugged. I see things much more clearly and differently. I understand things on a deeper level. I released my ego and pride and gained humility and gratitude. I forgave and let go of things of the past. I have been given a renewed mind, spirit and purpose. I am able to move forward, unencumbered by my past and previously held limiting and untrue beliefs about myself, people and life.

I have obtained a new life and a transformed mind that is Jesus seeking, positive, purposeful, and prolific. I am grateful to be in existence in this space and time, so I can be of service to God and His children, by fulfilling the purpose He charged me with. I am who I am, because God loved me enough to call me, save me and change me. As God changed me, I found myself thinking in ways that I never thought

I would. I began to act in ways that was foreign to me. As a matter of fact, I found myself responding to people and situations in ways that boggled my mind.

If anyone would have told me that I would turn to God to solve every issue and non issue in my life, I would not have believed them. But, not only has my faith in my Father grown, I too have grown. However, my road to salvation was not paved in gold or butterfly kisses. It was paved with pain, grief, suffering, anger, betrayal and hopelessness. Before I met the me I always hoped to be, I had to live the life of the old unsaved, broken and sinful me. All my life I felt as if I was fighting a battle that was unwinnable.

It was a battle that I later found out wasn't really even mine, but it was a product of the sins in and of this world. I had been in this battle before I came out of my mother's womb. This may sound crazy but from an early age I felt different but I didn't know why. As a child and up until 2013, I had many instances where I should have died. However, I was consistently saved in ways that had no other explanation, except by the grace of God.

God has been snatching me from the grip of death my entire life. There is no way that anyone can convince me that I am not destined for something. That He does not have a plan for me. If He didn't, I wouldn't be here. I know this because there were far too many opportunities for death to take me but it couldn't because God said "NO".

The old me had to deal with the blows of life: childhood sexual abuse, physical abuse, mental abuse, spiritual abuse, rape, abandonment, attempted murder, accidents, suicide, nicotine addiction, substance abuse, depression, brokenness, low self worth, low self confidence, anger, despair and more. It's not easy sharing with the world my brokenness. But, it was a part of my old life. It is to show that God can meet you wherever you are.

43

I wasn't fixed when I cried out. Lord knows I didn't even know where to begin at that point. Heck, I was at the lowest point I had ever been in my entire life. I did the only thing I could muster up to do at that point. I screamed, "HELP!" He had no problem stepping in and meeting me in the midst of my mess. God met me in my mess, looked around and said, "You ready?" In that moment, Jesus began the work of cleaning house. In the midst of my pain, brokenness and darkness, Jesus came in and met me where I was. This is what's called "Grace". He covered me and showed me what real love looked and felt like. I had never felt so loved, cared for and protected, in my entire life. My testimonies are as numerous as they are profound. Trying to explain with earthly words what God did and still continues to do for me, is limiting. But if I had to find one word to describe it, it would be AWESOME.

Looking back to where I've been, thinking about what Jesus has brought me through and looking forward to where God is taking me, leaves me in a state of awe and amazement. I am so grateful that He is nothing like man. Jesus covered me with His blood, love and light. Because of who He is and what He has done, I am saved, I am healed, I am whole and I am changed forever.

GOD IS DOING A MIGHTY WORK IN ME AND IN MY LIFE.

CHAPTER 10

CHANGE BECOMES ME

CHAPTER 10

POEM: CHANGE BECOMES ME

God is doing a mighty work in me and in my life.

When God creates change, it lasts forever.

God is transforming my life and I will never be the same.

God has blessed me, so I can bless others.

God has shown me love, so I can show love to others.

God has forgiven me, so I can forgive others.

God has given me understanding, so I can pass it on.

God has changed me, so I can change the world.

This is how I know, that change becomes me.

~ Gail A Henry-Walker ~

I BEGAN WORKING ON A PROJECT THAT HAS LITERALLY
BEEN 43 YEARS IN THE MAKING

CHAPTER 11

THE MESSAGE #1: NAKED AND EXPOSED

CHAPTER 11

THE MESSAGE #1: NAKED AND EXPOSED

Hebrews 4:13King James Version (KJV)- 13 Neither is there any creature that is not manifest in his sight: but all things are naked and opened unto the eyes of him with whom we have to do.

Almost a year ago I began working on a project that has literally been 43 years in the making. This project is one of those "life purpose" projects and if you've undertaken one of these you'll know exactly what I'm talking about. It's the type of project that moves you further away from just existing and towards living the type of life that moves and changes the world around you. These projects are God given and rarely are the ones we'd choose for ourselves.

What I viewed as a project, is more than a project; it's a ministry that is focused on waking up others, telling the world about how Jesus has impacted my life, spreading God's word, teaching spiritual oneness, teaching and showing unconditional love, and building up God's people.

If anyone would have told me that God would have called me into a teaching ministry, I would have laughed you into oblivion. That's how God operates though, isn't it? He creates each of us uniquely with a plan and a purpose that's so much bigger than we can comprehend.

My purpose is to minister to people who are confused, blocked and unsatisfied; those silently suffering in pain, those struggling with depression and hopelessness by turning their eyes to Jesus, the only one who can bring healing and restoration in their lives. Through Jesus we are able to see the effects of sin in our lives, the unhealthy patterns of thinking and behavior that have slowly grown up in our lives because of the influence of our own sin or the sins of others. Through Jesus we are able to break free from the bondage of sin! Jesus can and will do a mighty work in our lives. He will make us into a new creation. Listen to the promise for us in *Ezekiel 36:26, "I will give you a new heart and put a new spirit in you; I will remove from you your heart of stone and give you a heart of flesh".*

God can tell you who you really are because He created you! Only He can speak into your life the truth of who He created you to be. Only God can change you from the person you are now, into the person He created, the real authentic you! When Jesus transforms our lives and we are transformed into the person God created in HIS OWN IMAGE, we will finally experience the redemption, healing and forgiveness; the joy, peace, and hope; the strength, passion, and purpose we've been longing for.

It is my time to step into God's light, His truth, and my purpose. I will stand boldly in God's truth naked and exposed, with openness and love. - Gail A Walker

I wanted to give my family and friends a heads up. Think of this as my coming out party. I want to re-introduce myself to all of you.

Habakkuk 2:2-3King James Version (KJV) - 2 And the Lord answered me, and said, Write the vision, and make it plain upon tables, that he may run that readeth it. 3 For the vision is yet for an appointed time, but at the end it shall speak, and not lie: though it tarry, wait for it; because it will surely come, it will not tarry.

It has taken me 43 years of searching to recognize and understand God's purpose for me. That's a long time to search for one's purpose in life. What I've realized is the process of searching prepared me for

49

the destination of recognizing and understanding God's purpose for my life. All the trials I've faced, lessons I've learned, and struggles I've walked through, God has allowed all of those things to take place in my life and will use them to build His Kingdom.

I'm putting all those moments of my life on display, so that God can use them to grow you as He has used them to grow me! Everything God has given me, my talents and abilities, I lay before God as a sacrifice of worship, so that His Kingdom will be built here on earth.

Romans 12:2King James Version (KJV)- 2 And be not conformed to this world: but be ye transformed by the renewing of your mind, that ye may prove what is that good, and acceptable, and perfect, will of God.

Everything we need to live a life of purpose and joy, and life that builds God's Kingdom, has been made available to us. For 43 years everything I needed for life was right in front of me but I could not grasp it. It wasn't until He called me and I gave my life completely over to Him, that I was able to see the truth. My eyes were opened when God transformed my life and renewed my mind! It took me a while to arrive here, to the place where I know truth and purpose, but God had my arrival planned. He has brought me to this moment in time and prepared me to be useful and effective as a Kingdom builder.

Ha, I like to call those 43 years a very long incubation period, and I'm excited to share with you all that He's been teaching and showing me. I hope that what I have to share with you, the truth that God has taught me will change your life as it has changed mine.

Hebrews 5:12-14King James Version (KJV)- 12 For when for the time ye ought to be teachers, ye have need that one teach you again which be the first principles of the oracles of God; and are become such as have need of milk, and not of strong meat. 13 For every one that useth milk is unskilful in the word of righteousness: for he is a babe. 14 But strong meat belongeth to them that are of full age, even those who by reason of

use have their senses exercised to discern both good and evil.

My life, my struggles, my challenges, my sorrows, my circumstances, my tests and my lessons is what God will use to teach me, to change me from the inside out. God has used my past to show me, to prove to me, that He can change my future. I offer my life to you as a living testimony of His love, redemption, grace, forgiveness, resurrection and power to break the generational curse of sin.

I can't tell you why God has chosen me, but I can tell you that I am going to be obedient to do the work He has commanded me to do. I'm giving all that I have to the One who gave everything for me, to follow the path He lays before me and allow Him to fulfill the plan He has for my life. I am changed because of Christ. He saved me and delivered me from people, circumstances, patterns, and bondages I never thought I would be freed from. He freed me from sin! I am and will forever be grateful to Him, my God my Father.

2 Corinthians 10:3-5King James Version (KJV) - 3 For though we walk in the flesh, we do not war after the flesh: 4 (For the weapons of our warfare are not carnal, but mighty through God to the pulling down of strong holds;) 5 Casting down imaginations, and every high thing that exalteth itself against the knowledge of God, and bringing into captivity every thought to the obedience of Christ;

He stirred in me the changes that were needed for my yokes, shackles, chains, burdens, fallacies, and secrets to be unearthed, exposed and broken. He freed me from curses I was born into, curses that I could not break free of by my own might! If I wanted my life to change, I had to allow Jesus to do it.

Psalm 121:1-2King James Version (KJV) - 121 I will lift up mine eyes unto the hills, from whence cometh my help. 2 My help cometh from the Lord, which made heaven and earth.

True and "Permanent Life Change" is achieved slowly but steadily. It cannot be rushed and it can't be ignored. Life is a perpetual state of change. There will be times when your faithfulness to God will be tested. You'll find yourself in dark places, under attack by the evil one, tempted to sin, to give in to doubt and despair. Allow Christ to strengthen you and be obedient to the Holy Spirit's leading in your life. When you do fall, reach up to Christ, allow Him to pull you up, dust you off, and set your feet on solid ground.

The promise of the cross is that we never have to be alone again! Listen to the words of our savior Jesus Christ… *John 14:15-19 King James Version (KJV) - 15 If ye love me, keep my commandments. 16 And I will pray the Father, and he shall give you another Comforter, that he may abide with you forever; 17 Even the Spirit of truth; whom the world cannot receive, because it seeth him not, neither knoweth him: but ye know him; for he dwelleth with you, and shall be in you. 18 I will not leave you comfortless: I will come to you. 19 Yet a little while, and the world seeth me no more; but ye see me: because I live, ye shall live also.*

You are not alone. The Holy Spirit lives in you. You are not alone. He is above you and below you. You are not alone. He carries you when you can't walk any further. You are not alone. He cradles you when life becomes unbearable. You are not alone. He'll push you when you become too comfortable. You are not alone. Once you accept Jesus as your Lord and personal Savior, you will never be alone again. If you are not experiencing Him, then I will only say that you must be willing to allow Him to renew your mind. I promise if you choose Jesus and let Him do a wonderful work in you, what you'll receive at the end of the journey is priceless.

"The Spirit of the Lord GOD is upon me; because the LORD hath anointed me to preach good tidings unto the meek; he hath sent me to bind up the brokenhearted, to proclaim liberty to the captives, and the opening of the prison to them that are bound; To proclaim the acceptable year of the LORD, and the day of vengeance of our God; to comfort all that mourn; To appoint unto them that mourn in Zion, to give unto them

beauty for ashes, the oil of joy for mourning, the garment of praise for the spirit of heaviness; that they might be called trees of righteousness, the planting of the LORD, that he might be glorified." Isaiah 61:1-3

Everything I once was, everything I am, and everything I will become is on display. I am exposed, naked and unafraid. I hope that those of you, who knew me, can let go of who I was and see me for who I am now and who I will become. I … just like you, am more than my past and my future will be more than my present.

There are two things you can do to change the course of your life. First, you can accept Jesus Christ as your lord and personal savior and second, you can seek out the necessary assistance and tools to ensure you assist Christ, instead of impeding Him as He transforms you into His image.

Asking for and accepting help from others is a choice, much like the choice we make to turn to God and accept the help and healing He offers to all who are broken. The choice is yours to make but its my prayer that you will make the choice that leads you to being transformed more and more into the image of Christ.

I HAVE OFTEN PONDERED ON THE QUESTION OF "WHY
AM I HERE?" WHY IS MY LIFE FILLED WITH SO MUCH PAIN?
WHY DO I FEEL SO EMPTY?

CHAPTER 12

THE MESSAGE #2: PORTAL OF MY MIND

CHAPTER 12

PORTAL OF MY MIND

Luke 6:38 (NIV) Give, and it will be given to you. A good measure, pressed down, shaken together and running over, will be poured into your lap. For with the measure you use, it will be measured to you.

Hi, and welcome into the portal of my mind ... I have often pondered on the question of "Why am I here?" Why is my life filled with so much pain? Why do I feel so empty? I don't know about anyone else, but I can tell you, I have asked myself these questions time after time all throughout my life.

I wanted to know my purpose. I wanted to know why I had to go through all of these trials, tests, and struggles in my life. I wanted to know what it all meant. I wanted to know ... I wanted to know ... I wanted to know! Time after time, situation after situation, it made me want to know even more.

I always had a sense that there was more, that there were unseen things at play. I just didn't understand. I always said that "everything in life happens for a reason" and that "everything happens exactly the way it's supposed to happen" but that truth still didn't answer my questions.

All I knew was that, regardless of my circumstances, I felt empty, small, and insignificant. I knew I wasn't doing what I was supposed to be doing or feeling how I should be feeling. This just left me more dissatisfied. I had a yearning to do what I was supposed to be doing, to feel the way I wanted to feel, but had no idea how to achieve that.

My life was filled with upheaval, drama, unwelcomed situations, circumstances and pain ... so much pain. Don't get me wrong, my life was not without many great experiences and memories, they were just fleeting by. I couldn't grab hold of them. I didn't know why, all I knew was that no matter how hard I tried, I just couldn't.

The day my marriage came to a very abrupt and painful end was the moment that changed my life forever. One of the worst, most painful time of my life turned out to be the best thing that has ever happened to me. It was the day that I turned from myself and looked to God for help.

I fell on my knees and prayed like I had never prayed before. I asked God to watch over me, to guide me, to protect me, to ground me into dust and build me into the person He created me to be. That was the moment that God began to transform me from who I was into who I am becoming! This transformation took me through many dark valleys, deep ditches, and hidden realms. When the first phase of my long journey ended, I found that God had gently laid me in a place of great peace and even greater understanding.

It was in this place that God was finally able to do a great work within me, to rebuild me. Day by day I noticed changes within myself. While God did His part, I did mine. I developed tools that would assist me through my change. I began my research, read books, listened to CD's, and created my own (workbooks/worksheets/affirmations/ videos/voice recordings, and more) to use during my time of healing and transformation.

I was determined, with God's help, to create changes within myself. Although I had complete and unwavering faith that God was doing a great work in me, I had to do my part and work alongside Him! I wasn't helping God and I understood that. Why? God does not need assistance. I was working alongside God to help myself! If I was un-willing to put in the necessary work into myself, I would not have had the level of appreciation I should have when God was finished with me. I knew I had to actively take part in the process.

***Please Note ***

God is still working on me and He will continue until the day I cross over.

The understanding I received after my rebirth and commitment to change is what led to this book and many more to come, Gail A Henry, Coach and LGT Media Group, LLC and its SBUs and subsidiaries. From the moment of my re-birth, I began to live God's truth. God gave me beauty for ashes. I don't view the time it took me to arrive here as long, I view it as God's "Perfect Timing". I reached my destination when I was supposed to reach it, when God knew I was ready. I now knew my purpose. I also gained an understanding of why I had to endure so much pain.

God allowed me to go through great pain, so He could take me through all of it, to make me a living testament to His Grace, Greatness, Love, Power, Forgiveness, Redemption, and Restoration. He knew what I did not. I am here to help others who are suffering, confused, blocked and unsatisfied, those suffering in pain silently, those that are depressed, and those that feel hopeless. I am to use the understanding He gave me to help others. I went through all those things in order to bring you the tools you need to help yourself and to also open yourself up to God and His goodness if you so choose. Ultimately, turning to God is a CHOICE.

God is a generational curse breaker, a peacemaker, a peace giver, a thirst quencher, a restorer, an optimist, a forgiver, a joy giver, a redeemer, a healer, a provider of hope, a love magnet, and so much more.

Every morning before my feet hits the ground I say a prayer. This is my way of letting my Father know that He comes first. I am just grateful for all the wonderful blessings He has provided, He is providing, and those He has in store for me in the future. I love Him more today than I did yesterday and tomorrow I will love Him even more.

If any of my books, products, businesses and websites positively affects even one person in this vast universe, then I have fulfilled my purpose.

There are two things you can do to change the course of your life. You can accept God as your lord and personal savior and you can get the necessary assistance and tools to ensure you assist and not impede Him during your transformation.

Asking for and accepting help from others is a choice, much like the choice we make to turn to God and accept the help and healing He offers to all who are broken. The choice is yours to make but it's my prayer that you will make the choice that leads you to being transformed more and more into the image of Christ.

TEN YEARS AGO, I ASKED GOD TO COME INTO MY LIFE AND TAKE THE REINS. I WAS IN A PLACE OF BROKENNESS AND GREAT PAIN.

CHAPTER 13

THE MESSAGE #3: GOD TOOK THE REINS

CHAPTER 13

THE MESSAGE #3: GOD TOOK THE REINS

"For I know the plans I have for you, declares the Lord, plans for welfare and not for evil, to give you a future and a hope." Jeremiah 29:11

Ten years ago, I asked God to come into my life and take the reins. I was in a place of brokenness and great pain. But, from that day forth, He began to mold me, transform me, refine me, and rebuild me. As I walk along my path, I have learned that I have to be obedient to Him, to walk on the path that Christ has for me.

Things that He asked of me often didn't make any sense to me. He would send me places and I'd feel as if I was going backward not forward. The situations God allowed me to be placed in seemed like tests I was unprepared for. At times, my challenges and tests felt more like punishments than opportunities for Christ to grow me. Imagine doing what you were told to do and still getting in trouble! That's what following Christ felt like to me.

James 1:12 (NIV) "Blessed is the man who perseveres under trial, because when he has stood the test, he will receive the victor's crown, the life God has promised to those who love him."

Halleluiah! If you do not go through the trials, tests, and lessons in life and come out on the other side, you cannot get the victor's crown. No one receives a prize for not competing! If you decide to give up, sink into despair and stay there you can't get the victor's crown. I don't know about anyone else, all I knew was that I wanted that crown...I needed that crown...I was desperate and desperate people will do whatever it takes to get that crown. The victor's crown in this instance was my salvation.

When times such as these are upon us, God asks us to place our trust in Him and have faith that His way is always right. We need to get up, praise God, and ask Him to help us through it. I came to understand something when God placed me in a situation that caused me to be still and quiet before Him. I found out that the people, situations and circumstances that were placed on my path, unbeknownst to me at the time, had been placed there on purpose. They were there to help strengthen me and craft me into an OVER COMER and a VICTOR instead of what I had been for far too long ... a victim.

Everything that God placed into my life was placed there so that He could strengthen me on the inside. I discovered strength God had placed deep inside of me that I didn't know existed. I discovered many things inside of me I didn't know existed. Day after day I saw marked changes in my life. Now understand that I am not talking about the outer life. I'm talking about my inner life. I was being changed from deep within.

"I am crucified with Christ: nevertheless I live; yet not I, but Christ liveth in me: and the life which I now live in the flesh I live by the faith of the Son of God, who loved me, and gave himself for me." Galatians 2:20

It took me a while to understand that God was refining me. He was creating an awesome jewel out of me. *For You have tried us, O God; You have refined us as silver is refined. You brought us into the net; You laid an oppressive burden upon our loins. You made men ride over our heads; We went through fire and through water, Yet You brought us out into a place of abundance. Psalms 66:10-12*

Everyone who is crucified with Christ is being refined! I had to be placed in the refiner's fire, my impurities burned away, molded and prodded, shaped and changed. But thank you Jesus, when He was done with me, a new creation emerged to be marveled at.

"Therefore if any man [be] in Christ, [he is] a new creature: old things are passed away; behold, all things are become new." 2 Corinthians 5:17

I am a new creation. Christ didn't have to save me, He didn't have to deliver me, He didn't have to change me, but He did it anyway. Why? Because that's the kind of God He is. He is patient, kind, loving, tender, forgiving, merciful and full of grace.

You see, God took my broken, tattered, worn-out, ungrateful, disease ridden heart and gave me a heart that was filled with unfathomable, unconditional love. Through Him I am empowered. He gave me peace, faith, redemption, reconciliation, restoration, and understanding that I could never have achieved without Him. He placed people, circumstances, and situations along my life's path to teach, build and change me. He gave me the strength to accept His gifts and I pray that whatever He has in store for me, I will get the pleasure of using all these gifts to magnify and glorify His name and His Kingdom.

I am not perfect. I am not a Pastor, Minister, Bishop, Religious Leader, or Spiritual Guru. I am but a humble servant and student of Jesus. I don't know what God's plan is for me or how He is going to use me. But, my request to Him was this: I asked Him to bless me with the power of healing; I asked Him to use me to further His kingdom; And, I told Him that I would do whatever He asked of me. I yearn for the day where I will be able to utter the words *"…Why did you seek Me? Did you not know that I must be about My Father's business?" Luke 2:49*

With every fiber of my being I knew that day was drawing nigh and I had to prepare for the task Christ has called me to complete. I had to move past my many fears, my own reasoning, my doubts, and the voices of my inner critics. I had to allow God to break strongholds that were on me, within me and in my life. I had to allow Him to break me free of generational curses that were not mine to bear.

"The LORD [is] longsuffering, and of great mercy, forgiving iniquity and transgression, and by no means clearing [the guilty], visiting the iniquity of the fathers upon the children unto the third and fourth [generation]." Numbers 14:18

The devil is a liar. His strongholds had to be broken in the name of Jesus. Left and right, east and west, and north and south the enemy would have to flee out of the Lord's sight. His reign of terror over me and my life had to come to a swift and abrupt end. Halleluiah! God had to throw out a lot of "STUFF" I carried around inside of me my whole life. It permeated and tainted every aspect of my life from childhood up to the day of my deliverance.

How I survived life that way I have no idea. Seeing where I am now and knowing where I came from causes me to be in complete awe of God's magnificence. He is worthy to be magnified and praised all day every day, every minute and every second. To Him I scream "Glory"!

I had to ask for forgiveness from Him and myself because of how long it took me to put my complete trust in Him. But God works everything for our good because I have been to the pits of hell and now I'm here in "Jesusdom", and let me tell you the air up here is "Amazing". I had to go through some things but without those things I would not be me. I would not have the level of appreciation that I have for what God has done in my life, and I would not be able to fulfill God's purpose for my life.

I know I am not perfect but God's not looking for perfect people; He's looking for people He can perfect! Although He told me that I was wonderfully made. *"I will praise thee; for I am fearfully and wonderfully made: marvelous are thy works; and that my soul knoweth right well." Psalm 139:14.* God can and will use me despite of and because of my imperfections. It's those imperfections that make me perfect for the plan He has laid out before me. God has done and is still doing a great and mighty work in me, on me and outside of me.

And, I am a testament to His love, mercy, grace, resurrection, and power to save. Whatever He places on my heart to do or say, I will do it despite any underlying fears I may encounter. I am His and He is mine and so I am blessed and protected. *"For he shall give his angels charge over thee, to keep thee in all thy ways." Psalm 91:11*

Who's holding the reins in your life? Is it you or God?

There are two things you can do to change the course of your life. First, you can accept Jesus Christ as your lord and personal savior and second, you can seek out the necessary assistance and tools to ensure you assist Christ, instead of impeding Him as He transforms you into His image.

Asking for and accepting help from others is a choice, much like the choice we make to turn to God and accept the help and healing He offers to all who are broken. The choice is yours to make but its my prayer that you will make the choice that leads you to being transformed more and more into the image of Christ.

DEATH, DIVORCE, ABANDONMENT,
SEPARATION OR BREAK-UP.

CHAPTER 14

THE MESSAGE #4: GOD NEED YOU TO BE OKAY WITH BEING ALONE

CHAPTER 14

THE MESSAGE #4: GOD NEED YOU TO BE OKAY WITH BEING ALONE

This is a message for those that have or are experiencing the pain from the death of a loved one; those experiencing or have experienced a divorce; those who have been or feel as if they have been abandoned; those going through a period of separation; and those going through a break-up.

I would like to take a moment to pray and ask God to move our hearts to be receptive to His word and ask that He provide healing to those who are in pain. Dear Heavenly Father, I come before you with great thanks. Thank you for giving us another opportunity to experience another day. Thank you for all the wonderful blessings you have given us, the blessing of your presence in our lives, and the future blessings you have in store for us.

Father, I ask that the message you placed on my heart will provide healing to those who need it. I ask that their hearts are receptive, even in the midst of their pain and circumstances. Father I ask that you reach out to each and everyone who needs healing and touch their hearts, calm their spirits and quiet their minds so they can hear and receive this message Father. I ask that you step into their situations and provide a supernatural healing and covering to all those who need it. In Jesus' name I pray. -Amen

"He heals the brokenhearted and binds up their wounds." Psalm 147:3

I want to talk to you about what God wants us to do with our lone-liness. There will be times in life when we end up alone. You can feel alone whether you are single or have a life full of meaningful relation-ships. In your aloneness, don't panic or feel as if you are less than. I can tell you that I have been exactly where some of you are right now. You may feel broken, ashamed, betrayed, and filled with great pain and self doubt. Understandably, it's easy to fall into a "poor me" state when we are hurt and that has the potential to quickly get out of hand if not placed in Jesus' hands. Why did this happen to me? How could they do this to me? What did I do to deserve this?

"I have said these things to you, that in me you may have peace. In the world you will have tribulation. But take heart; I have overcome the world." John 16:33"

Although it's understandable, we've been called as followers of Christ not to dwell in a "poor me" state and get trapped there. Some of us have been trapped in this state for years, for some it's a fresh hurt, and for others it's become the pattern of your life. No matter how hard you try to shake it off, it seems to be a recurring theme. When you find yourself hurt and alone, you return to the self-focused place of "poor me". When we find ourselves saying "poor me" God wants us to take the focus off of ourselves and look to Him for guidance, strength and assistance.

I am here today to let you know that God "CAN" pull you out of this pattern once and for all. You can have this stronghold broken in your life. God can make you an overcomer; through Him you can overcome any eventuality that may arise in your life. Do you under-stand what that means? It means that even if a divorce, a death, a loss, a separation, or chaos is imminent you can trust that God will work out all these things for the good!

"And we know that all things work together for good to them that love God, to them who are the called according to [his] purpose." Romans 8:28

Whether you are alone or surrounded by people who love you; single or together with the one you love; you will be okay. After the trauma of a breakup you can rebound quicker, healthier, stronger, and filled with peace. Justifiably, after the chaos of a breakup, it's easy to feel alone, inadequate, and broken. In an attempt to escape the pain and rejection you feel, you might jump right into another relationship, hoping to find healing there. Even when you are the one who ended the relationship, you may see yourself respond in this way. You may try to distract yourself through destructive behaviors that turn into addictions. It's easy to be entrapped in worldly thinking; to end up stuck in a mind full of sorrow, grief, self-pity and doubt.

It's understandable. You are hurting and you need time to process your feelings and grieve the loss of something or someone that was important to you. Keep in mind, processing your feelings and working through grief isn't the same thing as getting stuck in your pain. If you focus on your pain instead of focusing on the one who provides a way out, you will find yourself stuck in your pain and grief. "Is any among you afflicted? Let him pray. Is any merry? Let him sing psalms." James 5:13

Guess what?

- You do not have to be alone.
- You do not have to reach for a person, place, or thing that can't fill you up or heal your pain.
- You do not have to wallow in self pity and doubt.
- You do not have to fill your life up with noise and distractions.
- You do not have to feel worthless.
- You do not have to feel unworthy.
- You do not have to feel ashamed.
- You do not have to go it alone!

You see, God wants to walk with you through the storm, through the pain in your life. God wants to be your first-love! When life looks and feels great, God wants to walk with you. When life is filled with struggles and pain, God wants to walk with you. Regardless of your life situation, God wants to be your everything. He wants you to know that He is all you need. That He, and He alone, is sufficient for every need of your heart.

God wants to fill us up. He wants you to give Him the ashes of your life and in return, He will give you His beauty. God wants you to know that, in Christ, you are worthy of His love. God wants you to know that in the midst of your pain, your sorrow, your grief, your self-pity, and doubts that:

- He will, take on your burdens.
- He will, take on your pain.
- He will, take on your sorrows.
- He will, take on your grief.
- He will, take on your self-pity and doubts.
- He will, take it all on himself
  …and in return, and in return…Halleluiah!
- He will, replenish your soul.
- He will, fill up your spirit.
- He will, bring peace to your mind.
- He will, mend your heart.
- He will, still your doubts.
- He will, quiet your inner critic.
- He will, bring healing to your body.

He wants all of this for you. He wants to give you a supernatural healing. But before He can do that, He requires that we recognize that He, and only He, is "enough" for us. He wants to walk and talk with you. He wants to share His wisdom with you. He wants to plant seeds in you. He wants to spend quality time with you; beyond the distractions of everyday life, beyond the pain, and beyond another person or thing getting in His way. There are things in our lives that God must clean out. He's able to do this at a faster rate when we are alone and unattached. Reason being, we must rely fully on Him because there is no one else to turn to. This is when we often find ourselves ready for God to clean the house.

Allow Jesus to show you Satan's lies that you have accepted as truth in your life. They may not even be words spoken by you into your life. We take on and believe incorrect and negative words, lies about ourselves, spoken into and over us by others. Some of these lies have been ingrained in us from the time we were young. They have been around us and in us for so long that we don't even realize that these lies are driving our lives. They drive our thoughts, our actions and our feelings. These lies, that we've come to believe, need to be revealed to us and removed by the Holy Spirit, God's Spirit alive in our lives! We need to let God replace these lies with the truth of who we are in Christ.

" *Adjusting our thinking to Scripture is the foundation for "be[ing] holy in all we do." (1 Peter 1:15b)*

God sees us much differently than we see ourselves. Let Him deposit into you the truth about yourself. God wants you to be okay within your aloneness, He wants you to rely on Him, so He can do a mighty work on and in you, your life, and in your situation. He wants to be with you so He can reveal to you the secret place within the depths of your soul that only He can dwell within. He wants your time. He wants your undivided attention. He wants you to seek Him. He wants you to rely completely on Him for all your needs. He wants you to grow in your faith, to learn to trust Him with all things. It is in your brokenness and aloneness that God will make you into a new creation if you let Him.

He wants you exactly where He placed you. Alone, Perfectly and

Beautifully, Alone!

If you felt that this message was for you or you know someone that could gain from it, I ask that you please share it. I thank God for planting seeds in me so I can plant them in others.

I KNOW THAT SOMETIMES WHEN PEOPLE ARE SPEAKING
TO ME I SEEM TO GO OFF SOMEWHERE ELSE.

CHAPTER 15

LOST IN TRANSLATION

CHAPTER 15

POEM: LOST IN TRANSLATION

I know that sometimes when people are speaking to me,
I seem to go off somewhere else.
It's not something that I can control,
Nor is it something I can really help.
I don't know any other way to tell you what's happening,
But I will surely try my best to explain.

It's just that my mind and my attention are being overtaken,
Something inside of me is becoming awakened.
But to the outsider trying desperately to be heard and is vying for my attention,
It may seem that I don't think what they are trying to tell me is worth being mentioned.

I hope my words don't get misconstrued,
And I'm truly sorry if you think that I'm being rude.
You see, there isn't anything you are trying to tell me now that you can't tell me later,
My mind and my attention have been overtaken by someone and something far greater.

When He speaks, sometimes it's at the most inopportune time for others,
However, for me I am forever grateful because it's an honor.
When He seeks my attention He makes sure that He is being heard,
It's like He flips my switch to off so that I can hear every word.

It Was Good I Was Afflicted

As I listen intently to what He has to say,
It may seem to others like I'm in a whole other place.
But at the moment God decided to chimed in,
YOU became the distraction.
And He made sure that,
HIS words were not lost in translation.

~ Gail A Henry-Walker ~

WHAT MODE OF TRANSPORTATION DO YOU CHOOSE
TO USE TO GO THROUGH LIFE?

CHAPTER 16

THE MESSAGE #5: ELEVATOR, STAIRS OR BALCONY?

CHAPTER 16

THE MESSAGE #5: ELEVATOR, STAIRS OR BALCONY?

Elevator, Stairs, or Balcony? What mode of transportation do you choose to use to go through life? If you put things into this perspective would your decision making from this point be different? The way you go through life is much like your relationship with God … It's a choice. We allow our lives to be influenced by others and to be influenced by God, but the path we walk in life is ultimately our choice. We get to choose the path we are going to take to get us wherever we are supposed to get to.

Every day you make choices or your choices are made for you because of the past choices you have made in life. It's important that we are aware of the choices we are making and take time to prayerfully weigh out the outcomes of our choices. Just as the words we speak today become our lives tomorrow, so do our choices. By the time our choices catch up to us, more likely than not, we've forgotten the choices of the past. Since our future is a direct result of our choices today, wouldn't it be best to consider what the cost will be later down the road? How high of cost are you willing to pay?

Our choice for transportation; elevator, stairs, or balcony; determines whether we soar, descend, or plummet.

Elevator

When you choose to take the elevator, which is God's preferred mode of transportation for you, life will not be without its challenges and obstacles. However, He will be there every step of the way with you. He will go ahead of you, pave a way for you, and give you the strength and courage to meet and overcome any resistance. Taking the elevator means that you have willingly chosen Him, made Him King of your life, and committed yourself to following the blueprint for life He created and has laid out before you.

Everything you need to know to live a fulfilling, purposeful, and abundant life is already plotted out in His blueprint for life, the Bible. Look, God never promised us that our walk with Him was going to be an easy one or that it would be fun. Jesus made it clear to His disciples that life would be difficult for them because of their choice to follow Him! God has promised us that:

- He would be there to catch us before we fall.
- Help us up when we falter.
- He will forgive us when we succumb to sin.
- He will love us without conditions.
- He will provide everything we need to survive and thrive.
- He will be at work in our lives, strengthening and encouraging us to live for Him.

These are all things He does for us when we believe in His son Jesus, put our faith in Christ as our Lord and Savior, and live in obedience to the Holy Spirit's leading in our lives.

Can you imagine the relief of not having to plan out your future and instead simply following the Holy Spirit's leading in your life today? Can you imagine how much more God would accomplish in your life, and how quickly He would accomplish it, if you would just turn your life over to Him? Can you imagine living a life where, in every struggle and storm, you are covered and protected by the God who rules over all the Heavens and the Earth? A life completely focused not on yourself but the God who created your life? A life spent with a best friend that will never leave you, forsake you, or give you horrible advice? Can you imagine that life? Man, that's Sweeeeet!

Stairs

When we choose to take the stairs, we choose to leave the path that God has called us to walk on. There are many obstacles, debris, distractions, unnecessary pain, spiritual warfare that we are ill prepared to fight. Sharp corners and turns, fear, suffering, stress, grief, highways to nowhere, greed, lust, affliction, loss of purpose, ego, pride, vanity, and idolism.

We may have started off strong with great intentions and expectations to follow God with our lives but life and people get us distracted. We begin to see things outside of God's path for our lives, pleasant things that tempt us to leave the path.

We allow Jesus to be our Savior but we stop allowing Him to be our Lord. We want Jesus to forgive us for our sins, we want Him to save us from the consequences of our sins, but don't want Him to be Lord. We leave the path God has called us to walk. We take a "shortcut" to get us what we want and find ourselves stuck in the consequences of sin.

Even with all of this, God is still there for you, can you imagine? He still loves you and wants to restore you, can you imagine? He still weeps for you, can you imagine? He still yearns for you, can you imagine? He died for you even knowing that you would turn your back on Him and sin, can you imagine? Even before you came to be, before you sinned, Jesus died on the cross so you could be forgiven of your sins! Even in the middle of your sin, God still graciously reaches out to you with forgiveness and restoration, can you imagine?

Balcony

We take the balcony when we remove God from His position as King of our lives and put ourselves in His place as King. The reality of the balcony is when God is taken off the throne of our lives, Satan takes his place and sin rules. When we choose to take the balcony, we are choosing life's roughest and bitterest path. Train wreck, 10 car pileup, massive explosion, nuclear blast, spiritual warfare on levels that will take divine intervention to be delivered from. Nothing but chaos, tyranny, oppression, bondage, shackles, turmoil, and grief of epic proportions, death, and destruction will lie in our wake.

Greed at the highest cost, who's gonna pay that? Lust of the flesh pulls us straight into darkness, who's coming to our rescue to light the way out? Lives shattered, who's going to put the pieces back together? And the idols come tumbling down, who shall stand up for us? Massive craters left in our wake, who's going to fill the void? Families destroyed, who's going to rebuild them? Life comes to an abrupt end, who shall be our restorer?

The Trinity, God the Father, God the Son and God the Holy Spirit that's who. For Him, nothing, nothing, nothing is impossible and everything is possible. Nothing and no one is beyond God's ability to redeem, restore, and repair!

Even after we turned our backs on Him He will mend our broken bones, did you know that? He will wage war against Satan on our behalf, did you know that? He will bring clarity after seasons filled with chaos, did you know that? He will break all shackles weighing us down and holding us back, did you know that? He will push back the darkness and light our way, did you know that? He will rebuild and restore us, did you know that?

It still amazes me that no matter what path you take in this life, no matter your choices, no matter your mistakes, no matter how great the sin, no matter how long repentance takes, God is always there when we are ready. God is in a perpetual state of pursuing our hearts and lives. God has always been and will always be in pursuit of you! An eternity of faithful pursuit of the hearts and lives of mankind has earned Him the name "The Hound of Heaven".

He is always behind us, always beside us, always before us, waiting for us to turn to Him, to turn our lives over to His care. Awake or asleep, God is in pursuit of our hearts, and will pursue us until we die and come face to face with Him on judgment day. Do you realize that God is constantly present in your life, waiting for you to acknowledge His presence and accept His invitation to be in relationship with Him?

So what mode of transportation have you chosen in the past? Have you been taking the elevator, stairs or balcony? Do you want to change course? Are you ready to change course? Will you choose to take the elevator?

Life does not have to be nor was it meant to be as difficult as we have made it. *There are two things you can do to change the course of your life. You can accept Jesus Christ as your lord and personal savior and you can get the necessary assistance and tools to ensure you assist and not impede Him during your transformation.*

BROKEN AT AN EARLY AGE BY MEN WHOSE INTENTIONS
WERE EVERYTHING BUT GOOD AND SINCERE, AS A CHILD I
LEARNED EARLY THAT I WAS NOTHING BUT A MERE TOOL.

CHAPTER 17

THE MESSAGE #6: THE BROKEN ONE

CHAPTER 17

THE MESSAGE #6: THE BROKEN ONE

Broken at an early age by men whose intentions were everything but good and sincere, as a child I learned early that I was nothing but a mere tool. Child abuse, rape, sexual abuse, physical abuse, mental abuse, spiritual abuse, secrets, neglect, terror, loneliness, fear, absence of love, unworthiness, worthlessness, and shame were the burdens I carried and wore like a badge. My circumstances, trials and tribulations became my identity. I am The Broken One.

My 1st Lesson: <u>God Can Heal Me</u> (*1 Peter 5:10 "But the God of all grace, who hath called us unto his eternal glory by Christ Jesus, after that ye have suffered a while, make you perfect, establish, strengthen, settle [you]."*) I wish I had known the truth of this verse as a child but I did not learn it until I experienced it. God taught me the truth of 1 Peter 5:10 as He healed me. If I had known of God's ability to heal, that little girl who was broken, would have put all her trust in God, believing that God could and would heal her.

You don't have to wait to put your faith in God, to believe in His ability and willingness to establish, strengthen, and settle you! Please don't hold on to the pain and hurt as long as I did. God wants to heal your hurts and strengthen you but He is waiting for you. He is waiting for you to put your faith in Him!

The darkness engulfed me. If I do more then surely I will be loved. If I become who you want me to be, then I'll feel loved. If I'm good then definitely you'll want me. If I do what you want me to do then maybe you'll save me. I'm invisible…I feel invisible. Can anyone see me?

What happened to my voice? I don't have a voice. I'm being smothered. I can't breathe! Will someone help me? I'm being silenced but I want to speak. Why do I have to wear these chains and shackles? What did I do wrong? Why am I here? I don't want to be here! I wish I was never born. Please I can't handle anymore. When will this all end?

I don't understand. I don't understand any of this. Why is this happening to me? I'm angry…so, so angry. I've become aggressive and intolerant. I've developed and perfected destructive behaviors. I've turned into a renowned secret keeper. Knowledge of God's love for me? … non-existent. Respect for the life God gave me … absolutely not. Paranoia … everyone and everything is against me. Fear… I will never be loved, wanted, or special.

What's stamped on my forehead? Why I'm a target for predators? Why do the people in my life always bring pain? Why me? Can anyone tell me why me? I'm so alone. I'm so worthless. I need someone to fix me. I need someone to help me. My life is out of control. I am the Broken One.

My 2nd Lesson: <u>Healing Requires Forgiveness</u> (*Ephesians 4:31-32 "31 Get rid of all bitterness, rage and anger, brawling and slander, along with every form of malice. 32 Be kind and compassionate to one another, forgiving each other, just as in Christ God forgave you.")* This was a hard lesson for me to learn and it took me over 30 years to do it. How do you get rid of the rage and bitterness and forgive those who have deeply hurt you? Forgiveness isn't easy but it is necessary. When we withhold forgiveness our lives remain broken, our minds remain in bondage to anger and pain, and joy is continually stolen away from us. When you forgive those that hurt you, you are released from the bondage their sin has over you. They will continue to live stuck in their sin but you are set free! You don't have to remain in bondage for so long like I did. God can and will set you free and He can do it in the midst of the chaos.

You will experience something amazing when God sets you free. You will see the people who hurt you differently. Your heart will break for the people who broke your heart. God will move you to a place where you will pray for their healing and restoration, for their freedom from bondage and sin! Forgiveness allows us to stop hating those who hurt us, and instead, love them like Jesus loves them!

I realized I couldn't fix myself alone and that only God could fix me. I turned to Jesus. I gave Him my ashes, I accepted His forgiveness, and I forgave myself and those that hurt me. I was finally ready to put down all the burdens that were never mine to carry. I gave Him the ashes of my broken life and in turn He gave me beauty.

My 3rd Lesson: <u>God Loves Me Enough to Heal Me</u> *(Isaiah 61:1- 3 "61 The Spirit of the Sovereign Lord is on me, because the Lord has anointed me to proclaim good news to the poor. He has sent me to bind up the brokenhearted, to proclaim freedom for the captives and release from darkness for the prisoners,[a] 2 to proclaim the year of the Lord's favor and the day of vengeance of our God, to comfort all who mourn, 3 and provide for those who grieve in Zion—to bestow on them a crown of beauty instead of ashes, the oil of joy instead of mourning, and a garment of praise instead of a spirit of despair. They will be called oaks of righteousness, a planting of the Lord for the display of his splendor.")* This is one of my favorite scriptures. It tells us about the great love that God has for us and His promise to heal and restore us. God grieves when we grieve. He hurts when we hurt. God doesn't just hurt for us … He hurts with us! God desires to take all of our pain and replace it with joy; to take our ashes and give us a crown of beauty. Cry out to God … Release your pain. God hears our cries. Trust in God's righteousness and justice. Allow God to deal with our enemies. Our job is to forgive and to leave the rest in God's hand.

Jesus filled me with love like I've never experienced. Jesus forgave all of my sins. God restored me to the person He created me to be. Jesus succeeded where the world failed me. Jesus loved me hard, healed me, completed me, gave me hope, gave me purpose, redeemed me, and has filled me up with spiritual goodness and light to the point of overflow!

Jesus created avenues of reconciliation between me and those who have caused me great pain and wronged me. Jesus restored my faith in Him and in His creation. Jesus showed me that man can never give me what He can. He showed me that although man failed and hurt me, God can redeem that pain and move me to fulfill His purpose for my life.

I am beautiful. I am loved. I give love freely and without conditions. I am wanted. I am needed. I am forgiven. I forgive without conditions! I am healed. God uses me to heal others. I am a servant to others. I have been reminded that I am filled with greatness and purpose.

My 4th Lesson: <u>God Wants to Pour Out His Love on Me</u> *(1 Timothy 1:14 "14 The grace of our Lord was poured out on me abundantly, along with the faith and love that are in Christ Jesus.") (Psalms 147:3 "He heals the brokenhearted and binds up their wounds.") (Jeremiah 31:3 3 The Lord appeared to us in the past, [a] saying: "I have loved you with an everlasting love; I have drawn you with unfailing kindness.")* Once I released my pain and gave it all to God He poured out love and blessing onto me that I didn't know existed. I will forever be grateful to my father. Let go and let God!

(Matthew 11:28-30 "Come to me, all who labor and are heavy laden, and I will give you rest. Take my yoke upon you, and learn from me, for I am gentle and lowly in heart, and you will find rest for your souls. For my yoke is easy, and my burden is light."). Letting go of the painful events of our past is difficult. It's easy to remain a victim and be victimized over and over again by our own mind and choices. It's much easier to hold on to the pain, hurt, and anger. But at what cost do we hold on? Is the price of keeping our ashes too high?

- If the price is growing increasingly bitter, then it's too high.

- If the price is remaining angry, then it's too high.

- If the price is living a destructive lifestyle, then it's too high.

- If the price is living in constant pain, then it's too high.

- If the price is our sanity, then it's too high.

- If the price is having no love for the person God created us to be, then it's too high.

- If the price is having no respect for our self or our bodies as God's creation, then it's too high.

- If the price is being trapped in hell on earth, then it's too high.

- If the price is continuing the cycle of abuse, then it's too high.

- If the price is remaining in abusive relationships or environments, then it's too high.

- If the price is living in a state of suspended animation, then it's too high.

- If the price is being paralyzed by addictions, then it's too high.

- If the price is our joy, then it's too high.

- If the price is not finding or living God's purpose for our lives, then it's too high.

- If the price is not knowing, finding, or giving love, then it's too high.

- If the price is living in constant fear, then it's too high.

- If the price is living in a perpetual state of shame, then it's too high.

- If the price is living a life void of forgiveness, then it's too high.

God can and will gladly take any and all ashes you bring Him. He will take the brokenness you present to Him and He will transform you into a thing of beauty to be marveled at. I am no longer The Broken One.

People and life may have left you feeling weak, unloved, and broken. However, you don't have to remain one of the Broken Ones. *There are two things you can do to change the course of your life. You can accept Jesus Christ as your lord and personal savior and you can get the necessary assistance and tools to ensure you assist and not impede Jesus during your transformation.*

THIS MESSAGE WAS PLACED ON MY HEART WHEN I WAS
HAVING A DIFFICULT TIME RECONCILING WHAT WAS
HAPPENING WITH A VERY IMPORTANT RELATIONSHIP I
HAD WITH A FAMILY MEMBER.

CHAPTER 18

THE MESSAGE #7: KNOW THY ENEMY

CHAPTER 18

THE MESSAGE #7: KNOW THY ENEMY

Put on the whole armor of God, that ye may be able to stand against the wiles of the devil. Ephesians 6:11

This message was placed on my heart when I was having a difficult time reconciling what was happening with a very important relationship I had with a family member. I could not understand what was happening between us until a calm soft voice kept telling me to look ... just look ... can't you see?

For we do not wrestle against flesh and blood, but against the rulers, against the authorities, against the cosmic powers over this present darkness, against the spiritual forces of evil in the heavenly places. Ephesians 6:12

As I looked at the person before me, screaming and cursing me; reaching into their arsenal and pulling out their preferred weapons and firing, bombing and nuking; the more they fired the more pleasure they got; the more hurt they inflicted the more powerful they felt. This person wanted to cause maximum pain. They wanted to murder me with their words and anger. They wanted to crush me. They wanted to demolish me.

The look on their face, the words from their lips were hurtful and disgusting, but all I could do was look in horror as tears fell down my face. I will never forget that day because it was the day that I finally was able to see how much power Satan has over those that are still sitting on the fence or in other words "Still Asleep". Those that are not awake and are teetering between following Jesus and being of this world don't realize that Satan can and will have his way with them whenever he pleases.

When he needs to bring down one of God's children he will use whomever he can to do it even your family, friends and those you love. These are the ones that hurt the most because it is someone you love that is trying desperately to bring you down. At first I threw up my defenses and went on the offensive because it was pure reflexes but I couldn't do it. I didn't know what to do so I did the only thing I could, I gave the situation up to God and carefully tried to pull myself out of the situation. The more I tried to extricate myself the more I was pursued.

Be sober-minded; be watchful. Your adversary the devil prowls around like a roaring lion, seeking someone to devour. 1 Peter 5:8

I can now recognize the devil when I see him and he was in rare form on this particular day. I immediately began to pray in my mind. I didn't want to respond in the same way this person was and to be honest I couldn't. I couldn't because I was no longer the person I once was who would have gone toe to toe and ultimately demolished this person. That would not have made me feel any better and it would not have helped the situation. God is good all the time. I thank Him for the changes He made in me.

I thank Him every day for accepting me when I asked Him to come into my life. I thank Him every moment because I was able to see the changes He was making as He was making them. I'm thankful because what He did for me is what's called "Deliverance". When you are delivered from things you don't have to second guess if something happened or if it worked. It is as clear as day that you have changed. You are still under construction, but major shifts are being experienced in your life when you have deliverance.

The thief comes only to steal and kill and destroy. I came that they may have life and have it abundantly. John 10:10

It won't matter what you want to still do or don't want to give up, when you get delivered from things you won't want to take any of those things back. Attitude...gone, addictions...gone, negative mindset... gone and the desire to afflict pain on another human being...gone. I am so grateful I am fully awake.

However, what do you do about the person that the devil is trying to use to get at you? The only thing I could do in that situation was to put on the whole armor of God and rebuke the devil and his trickery. Then I took ten steps back and placed Jesus in my place for Him to fight that battle and I walked away.

Even though this person thought they knew what they were doing they didn't really know and neither did they know who was leading the charge and why. They didn't even know they were being used and if I was to tell them it would only have made the situation more volatile. They are under the impression that it's all their doing. I, I, I, and I. All they can think about is their selves. I want, I need, I will, I don't...I. Figuring out who your real enemy is quickly, will save you a whole lot of grief. Even though it is a loved one it is important to look past their physical form. God has given each and every one of us a discerning spirit. Ask your spirit to show and tell you what's really going on at any given time.

I was not battling a loved one, on that day, I was battling the devil that was using my loved one to get at me. He wanted me to hurt someone that I loved so I could feel guilty. He wanted me to respond in kind to this person so God would be disappointed that I didn't do as I knew I should which is to immediately forgive them and myself and to pray and ask Him to solve this problem. This is how God expects His children to respond. How can you be a reflection of Jesus if we react or respond in the same way the other person is acting? We can't.

God never said that His way would have us smelling like roses all the time, but He did say that He would never leave us nor forsake us. When we need Him we can always call upon Him. I cannot say I handled the situation with complete finesse, but I know I didn't handle it in the way the devil had hoped. For that I say, "Oh yeah! Oh yeah!" He wanted me to fail the test but I didn't. He wanted me to curse them and in turn curse myself but I didn't. I was tested and I passed that test because I did not respond in the way the devil wanted me to.

I was then able to look back on my life and see how the devil not only used other people against me but how he used me against other people. The devil is cunning and deceitful, *and no wonder, for even Satan disguises himself as an angel of light. 2 Corinthians 11:14.* It is very important that we remain vigilant to what our true motives are and what or who is driving our desires and actions. It is easy to tell who is driving you. If it is positive, others centered and forwards God's kingdom, then you are being led by our Father. If it is negative, self centered and furthers earthly desires, then you are being led by sin and Satan will have his way with you whenever he wants because he can.

If you felt that this message was for you or you know someone that could gain from it, all I ask is that you please share it. I thank God for planting seeds in me so I can plant them in others. *There are two things you can do to change the course of your life. You can accept Jesus Christ as your lord and personal savior and you can get the necessary assistance and tools to ensure you assist and not impede Him during your transformation.*

AS TEARS FLOWED DOWN MY FACE I COULD NOT BELIEVE
THAT I WAS STILL HOLDING ONTO THOSE MEMORIES.

CHAPTER 19

THE MESSAGE #8: BLANKET FORGIVENESS

CHAPTER 19

THE MESSAGE #8: BLANKET FORGIVENESS

The other day I was speaking with a relative. As I answered a question they had asked I found myself in great pain as memories began to flood in as I spoke. As tears flowed down my face I could not believe that I was still holding onto those memories. I had no idea those moments in time were still causing me such great pain. At that moment, I realized that when I had forgiven the individual I was speaking about I had only forgiven them for one way they hurt me. I thought I had forgiven them for everything but really didn't.

I understand now that what I failed to do was to forgive that person for all the pain and hurt they had caused me. I should have given them and everyone else that I was holding grudges against, Blanket Forgiveness. Blanket Forgiveness? Yes!

In John 20:21-23 21 So Jesus said to them again, "Peace be with you; as the Father has sent Me, I also send you." 22And when He had said this, He breathed on them and said to them, "Receive the Holy Spirit. 23"If you forgive the sins of any, their sins have been forgiven them; if you retain the sins of any, they have been retained."

You see when you fully forgive, God's peace will rest upon you, and the Holy Spirit will comfort you. The forgiveness I was withholding was hidden deep inside. I had no idea that I was still holding on to it. When people continually hurt us and we simply move on without dealing with the hurt or forgiving them, we end up holding on to the old hurt. Then when they hurt us again that new hurt piles up on top of the old hurt, pushing those "old hurts" down. That old hurt becomes forgotten consciously. However, subconsciously it is far from forgotten. It festers inside of us and colors our life unbeknownst to us.

It affects our thoughts, actions & reactions, agendas, and all other areas of our life. We just don't realize it. The same thing happens when we don't forgive ourselves. The end result is fear, anxiety, colored views, apprehension, anger, negative thought pattern, grudges, mistrust, and more. That's a lot of stuff blocking us from receiving the fullness of God's love and blessings that He wants to give us. God requires us to free ourselves from unforgiveness.

When we choose to withhold forgiveness, we block God from doing what He desires to do in our lives. When we are unable to extend forgiveness to others we become unable to accept the forgiveness God extends to us and forgive ourselves. Let me say this again … If we cannot forgive we cannot readily accept God's forgiveness into our lives and forgive ourselves!

Why? It's simple, we won't think we are deserving of it.

We don't think He can really give it. We are holding on to all that pain and anger towards others and that pain and anger begins to take hold of us. It manifests itself in our lives and we become unable to see past that hurt and pain. We must let go! Let go of the hurts. Let go of the pain. Let go of the anger. Let go of the grudges. Let go of the negative thoughts. Shed no more tears because forgiveness has broken the hold they once had over you.

Through forgiveness you open the door for God to pour blessings into your life. Many times we can't remember old hurts and not because we've moved past them either. This is when you start from scratch and pray a prayer of blanket forgiveness. Ask God to move through the far reaching recesses of your mind and heart and cover them with the blanket forgiveness prayer. Ask God to remove all hurts, known and unknown, by forgiving all hurts known and unknown. Let God know that you forgive everyone for all hurts committed against you and forgive yourself for any hurts you caused to others.

Then ask God to forgive you for the sins you've committed against others, for the hurt you've caused in their lives, and to forgive all those whose sin has hurt you. Ask Him to bless them, keep them, shine His face upon them, and bring them peace. As you bless them so too are you blessed. As you curse them so too are you cursed.

Blanket forgiveness is a way for you to rid yourself once and for all of the things holding you back from fulfilling God's plan for your life. When I prayed that prayer I felt the presence of the Lord move through me. I felt a pressure build up in my lower back that wasn't there before and the pressure moved around my waist, through my pelvic area pushed itself out and then it was gone. My heart was so much lighter and I knew I was free. I thank God for freeing me from those shackles. When I sing no more shackles, no more chains…It means something to me. I am grateful that God revealed blanket forgiveness to me. I didn't know what it was but now I do and so it is now something that I use and teach to others.

ISAIAH 55:11 SAYS: SO SHALL MY WORD BE THAT GOES OUT FROM MY MOUTH; IT SHALL NOT RETURN TO ME EMPTY, BUT IT SHALL ACCOMPLISH THAT WHICH I PURPOSE, AND SHALL SUCCEED IN THE THING FOR WHICH I SENT IT.

CHAPTER 20

THE MESSAGE #9: SPEAK YOUR TOMORROW

CHAPTER 20

THE MESSAGE #9: SPEAK YOUR TOMORROW

Isaiah 55:11 says: So shall my word be that goes out from my mouth; it shall not return to me empty, but it shall accomplish that which I purpose, and shall succeed in the thing for which I sent it.

What will your future look like? What do you want it to look like? In your future, who are you? What are you like? How do you feel? Do you have a positive mindset or a negative one? What type of life are you living? Are you married or are you single? What does your family structure look like? How well do you get along with the people around you? Are you living a life of abundance or scarcity? Are you a champion or mediocre? Are you living a purposeful life or an empty one?

We should all ask ourselves these questions at least once in our lifetime and we should also have the answers to them or at least ones that we create in our mind. If we don't have a clear picture of what we would love our life to look like, how else can it be created? God has His own plan for our lives, but He never says that we are without a voice. We help create our future every day because we are co-creators. The words we speak today create our tomorrow. The thoughts that we keep today shapes our tomorrow. The actions that we take today become our results tomorrow.

Each day that passes is a tomorrow. So every day we are blessed with life, we can use it to propel us closer towards what we want, or push us farther away from it. I hate being…I'm never going to…I hate my … I can't stand my … I will never … That will never … And the list goes on and on and on. We waste so much time focusing on the negative things that we overlook all that is wonderful, good, and right.

We spend so much time focusing on all the things we don't like or don't want and far too little on the things that we do. We focus on all the things that we want instead of the things we already have. We yearn for that which is lost instead of cherishing that which we still possess. We spend a lot of time focusing on getting more of instead of appreciating and tending to what we have.

When you speak your future into existence, who is the beneficiary in the end? Is it just you or are others included? Are you being served or are you serving others? When you strive for wealth and attain it, will you keep all of it for yourself or use it to bless others? Look, how we think and what we think drastically affects our tomorrow. So think yourself into a future worth having.

If you find that most of your thoughts and words are negative and are in complete contradiction to the life you truly desire, then it is time to change your way of thinking, and the words you choose to speak into yourself and others. Your words can either lift you up or tear you down. Your thoughts can either cause you to feel good or horrible. When you change your thoughts you change your words and when you change your words you change your life.

Not many people are living the lives that they want, but they are living the life they created. The life we are living right now, for many of us, is the life we've created for ourselves. It matters not how great or horrible it is, we created it. I know you don't like the idea of this but it is the truth and not my truth but The Truth. There are things that God has ordained for us. Lessons He has for us and things He wants to accomplish through us, but we still get to choose to do it or not. When we live our lives speaking and thinking negatively all the time, nothing good can penetrate our lives, because we won't allow room for it.

People say a lot of things. They say they want a better life. They say they want to become this or that. And the things they want are accessible, even when unseen, but before they attempt to reach for it their next thought or words contradict and negate that which they spoke into being. That leaves confusion and chaos and that is exactly what will come towards you, sometimes at an accelerated rate. Wonderful thoughts and words give way to doubt, fear, confusion, apathy, procrastination, and stagnation.

You want to know how to change your tomorrow?

– Change the way you think.

– Choose the words you speak wisely.

– Put action behind your thoughts and words.

– Create a roadmap, a path marked out to get there.

– Do not allow fear and doubt to win out. It's okay to be afraid, but it's not okay to let it keep you from action. *(I'm not talking about anything that will put your life or the lives of others in danger.)*

If the words you are speaking into your life or the lives of others are not to elevate, inspire, or help, it does not need to be spoken. Paul tells us this in Ephesians 4:29:

Do not let any unwholesome talk come out of your mouths, but only what is helpful for building others up according to their needs, that it may benefit those who listen. (Ephesians 4:29)

If you have something to say that will be hard for you to say or for someone else to hear, choose your words carefully. Even difficult talks can be successfully achieved when approached with humility, dignity, and positivity.

We have to start being able to nourish ourselves. We self-nourish by speaking what we are to become into ourselves and our lives. However, we must also commit to speaking the same into others.

- Speak achievements into your life and the life of others.

- Speak blessings into your life and the life of others.

- Speak deliverance into your life and the life of others.

- Speak divine connections into your life and the life of others.

- Speak forgiveness into your life and the life of others.

- Speak gratitude into your life and the life of others.

- Speak growth into your life and the life of others.

- Speak healing into your life and the life of others.

- Speak hope into your life and the life of others.

- Speak humility into your life and the life of others.

- Speak joy into your life and the life of others.

- Speak life into yourself and into the life of others.

- Speak love into your life and the life of others.

- Speak opportunities into your life and the life of others.

- Speak positivity into your life and the life of others.

- Speak prosperity into your life and the life of others.

- Speak purpose into your life and the life of others.

- Speak rebirth into your life and the life of others.

- Speak reconciliation into your life and the life of others.

- Speak redemption into your life and the life of others.

- Speak restoration into your life and the life of others.

- Speak spiritual closeness with Jesus into your life and into the life of others.

- Speak success into your life and the life of others.

- Speak transformation into your life and the life of others.

Speak your tomorrow and speak it loud and clear. Then hold on to that and nothing else. Acknowledge and then let go of:

- The fear that tells you it cannot be achieved.

- The doubts that tell you that you are unworthy.

- Of thoughts that tell you it will never happen.

- Of ego and pride when things don't go right or the way you envisioned or anticipated.

- Of complete control and leave plenty of room for Jesus to take care of you, guide you and protect you.

Hold on to that which you desire your life to become and ask Jesus to guide you and light your path. Speak your tomorrow until your tomorrow becomes your today. Take a look at my "Speak Your Tomorrow" paradigm.

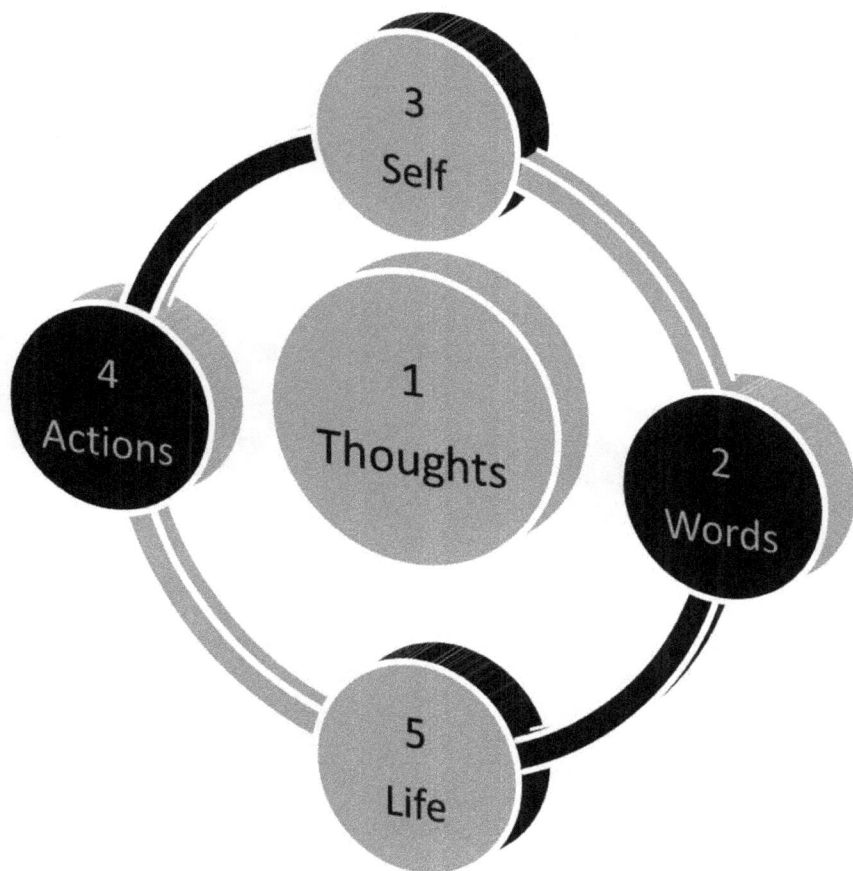

Change your life by creating a shift in your way of thinking. Once you create a shift in your thoughts, you've also created a shift with the words you speak. Once you create a shift with the words you speak, you create a shift within yourself. Once you create a shift within yourself, you create a shift in your actions. Once you create shift in your actions, you will have created a new life. Caution, make sure it is the life you truly want.

AS I PRAYED IN THE SPIRIT I ASKED FOR A SCRIPTURE
TO READ. I ASKED FOR JESUS TO PROVIDE ME WITH THE
UNDERSTANDING NEEDED TO SHARE THE TRUTH OF GOD'S
WORD WITH YOU.

CHAPTER 21

THE MESSAGE #10: FIX YOUR MIND, EYES AND LIPS ON JESUS

CHAPTER 21

THE MESSAGE #10: FIX YOUR MIND, EYES AND LIPS ON JESUS

As I prayed in the spirit one night I asked for a scripture to read. I asked for Jesus to provide me with the understanding needed to share the truth of God's word. There are changes happening all around me, and to keep myself centered in Christ I reach out to Jesus for guidance and wisdom. I asked God for a message for me and for those I love and what I received was oh so much more. At the end of my prayer He led me Job 1. Let me share what He told me with you...

Job 1 Living Bible (TLB) 1-22

1 There lived in the land of Uz a man named Job—a good[a] man who feared God and stayed away from evil. 2-3 He had a large family of seven sons and three daughters and was immensely wealthy,[b] for he owned 7,000 sheep, 3,000 camels, 500 teams of oxen, 500 female donkeys, and employed many servants. He was, in fact, the richest cattleman in that entire area.... You can visit Job in your bible to read the rest of the passage.

As I read the passage Jesus gave me this insight ... As children of God we really know how to praise Him when everything is going great. Woo Hoo! Halleluiah! Praise God! God you are good...all the time and all the time God you're good! We are quick to praise God when everything is great, its smooth sailing, without a cloud in sight.

But then comes a storm, from what seems like out of nowhere. Waters that were once calm and clear are now rough and muddy. We find ourselves in the middle of trials, tests, and struggles. It is in the middle of our trials, tests, and struggles that we find out just how committed we are to Christ.

- Job loss

- Terminal illness

- Unexpected death

- Sickness

- Endings

- Stagnation

- Divorce

- Separation

- Family issues

Whew…the list is endless.

- So now what?

- What do you do?

- What do you say?

- What do you think?

- Where do you look for answers to your many questions?

- Who do you blame?

Do any of these sound familiar?

- Why me Lord?

- What did I do to deserve this Lord?

- Father, how could you let this happen?

- Father, why have you left me?

- Father, can't you hear my cries?

- Father, are you going to help me?

- Father, why have you forsaken me?

- Father, why did you do this?

- Father, I thought you loved me?

Then the pressure gets more intense...and more intense...and more intense. Does any of this sound familiar?

- I don't want to go on.

- God I can't take anymore.

- I've had enough, stop now!

- How could this be happening if there is a God?

- God why are you punishing me?

- God I hate you!

- There is NO God!

We allow ourselves to be consumed by grief, worry, suffering, pain, anguish, fear of the unknown, fear of death, regret, and anger. In the grips of these feelings we lash out at God. We curse Him and His name. We turn our backs on Him and abandon Him. We become so consumed by our own suffering that we fail to respond like Job did. Job fell to his knees and in pain and grief He thanked God for giving him all that he had been given. He expressed gratitude for all he had been given, even though all those things had been removed and he was in great pain.

He understood the principle that things and people are only here for a set period of time. We have to understand that just as thankful as we were to get those things, we must also be thankful when they are taken away from us. These tests and trials are not without purpose.

They are here to test our resolve, our faith, our commitment, and our gratitude. Not for God's benefit but for ours! God knows how deep our faith runs. He knows exactly how we will respond to the trials, tests, and struggles in our lives. He knows what we have placed in front of Him. He knows, but we don't!

What God showed me was that I had made all these things, including my own life, more important than Him. Whatever we place above Christ, that idol we worship, will cause us great pain when it is taken away. We will be doubly hurt. Hurt while living under the curse of idolatry and hurt when our idols are torn away from us. When God removes those things we have placed above Christ we find ourselves empty. Trust me this is a painful experience. No matter what it is, whatever idol you have placed above Christ, you will crumble when it is removed, and feel great loss and emptiness.

- Spouse

- Children

- Wealth

- House

- Car

- Health

- Drugs

- Alcohol

- Sex

- Everything and anything ....

If you elevate anything above Jesus Christ you will be in for a world of pain. To curse Him and turn your back on Him because He has removed your idols, is to turn away from your only source of true comfort, salvation, and redemption. Only God is truly worthy of our worship because He offers to us what no created thing can:

- Hope

- Healing

- Grace

- Unfailing and Unfathomable Unconditional Love

- Forgiveness

- Joy

- Acceptance

- Restoration

- Redemption

- Reconciliation

- Peace that Surpasses All Understanding

- Blessings

- Favor

He should be our source of strength and the object of our worship. Through Him and with Him we can overcome anything Satan can throw at us. God loves us and promises to walk with us through our pain and suffering. He will go before us, light our path, and guide us. God always has a plan. Everything that happens good, bad, or indifferent, God is able to use that to accomplish His plan for our lives. Everything happens in God's timing, nothing happens in this world that God has not caused or allowed to happen! Even when our sin appears to make a mess of His plan, He always readjusts to make a new path to the destination He's always had planned for us.

Have faith and cast all your pain, troubles, and cares on Jesus. Then let go and let God! Daily ask Jesus to be faithful to His promise to provide for all your needs. Allow Him to guide you through every moment of your life. Life happens every day! There will always be something going on. Something unexpected will always happen. Christ calls us not to focus on what is happening in our lives but to fix our mind, eyes, and lips on Him.

The doctor tells you your illness is terminal. The one you love leaves you. Death takes a loved one away from you. Cry out to Jesus! Tell Him how much you need Him and how much you love Him. Tell Him how grateful you are for all the blessings He has provided, He is providing, and He will provide in the future. Tell Him how grateful you are to Him for the peace He will give you. Thank Him for the healing He has already given you. Thank Him! Thank Him! Thank Him! Thank Him! Send up praises to Jesus. Keep your mind fixed on Jesus through daily prayer, praise, and worship!

Stay in prayer. Stay in His presence. Maintain a grateful heart! It's great to praise Him in the good times but He wants us to praise Him when things have gone horribly awry. Do not focus on the problem, focus on your Savior! Christ desires to be our focus, to be our vision.

If your mind is consumed with your problems, what space is left for Him? Where does He fit in? How can Jesus provide you a way out of your problems when you're too busy trying to fix your problems yourself?

Where is the trust you said you had in Him? Where is the faith you thought you had in Him? Life is a virtual classroom and class is always in session! Every problem we face, every trial we struggle through, and every test laid before us will be used by God to draw us closer to Him and transform us into the image of Christ. I don't know about you but I want to pass all my classes. What about you?

Life, people, and things may have distracted you and drawn your focus off of Christ. Thank God we don't have to allow pride and ego to prevent us from turning back to God. Humble yourself and change your focus. *There are two things you can do to change the course of your life. You can accept Jesus Christ as your lord and personal savior and you can get the necessary assistance and tools to ensure you assist and not impede Jesus during your transformation.*

I'M NOT SURE WHY BUT I'VE BEEN FINDING MYSELF
AROUND PEOPLE THAT ARE PRETTY NEGATIVE.
THEIR THOUGHTS ARE NEGATIVE AND THEIR
ACTIONS ARE ALSO NEGATIVE.

CHAPTER 22

THE MESSAGE #11: GET YOUR MIND RIGHT - NEGATIVE MINDSET

CHAPTER 22

THE MESSAGE #11: GET YOUR MIND RIGHT - NEGATIVE MIND-SET

And be not conformed to this world: but be transformed by the renewing of your mind, that we may prove what is that good, and acceptable, and perfect, will of God. Romans 12:2

I'm not sure why but I've been finding myself around people that are pretty negative. Their thoughts are negative and their actions are also negative. Everywhere I turn I'm faced with negativity. It has become so much, that I find myself being affected, and I had to go into prayer and ask God to show me how I can be around this without it affecting me. We can't always escape negativity so learning how to deal with it was very important to me.

This world is filled with many bitter and scornful people. People are bitter and scornful for a multitude of reasons; loss, ending of relationships, abandonment and personal issues. But, our Father wants us to know that no matter what we go through in life we don't have to let our outside circumstances dictate how we feel on the inside. How we feel on the inside will undoubtedly reflect on the outside what our thought life looks like.

As I prayed I heard and saw three words; environment, group and food. What? Environment, group and food Lord? I said, "God, I don't get it!" He was so patient with me and I greatly appreciated that. He showed me how these things affect our mind, our body and our spirit. He showed me His truth and He gave me tools to deal with each of the three things.

Environment: Where We Spend Most of Our Time

Did you know that where we spend our time greatly influences how we think, feel and act? Whether it's our home, school, library, church, clubs and other places, what's taking place in it and the people within it influences us. God showed me how my environment affected me and what I needed to do to combat any negative influences that are prevalent.

No matter how badly we want to shrink away and sequester our self in a closet somewhere, that's just not feasible. We have to live and if we want to thrive we have to do something that sounds simple but is far from being simple. We have to renew our mind. We have to pay attention to our mind and change our patterns if our thoughts, words and actions align with the world around us. Remember, as Christians we are not to conform to this world.

The way to combat negative influences is not to run from the environment because we can't. No matter where we go there will be negative influences. This is why it is important to have a renewed mind.

Home Life: If our home life is hectic, unhealthy, troubled or filled with perversion and violence we can turn to God to "Be" the way out and to "Show" us the way out. And, if our prayers are not answered the way we want it to, don't think He has forsaken us, there may be something within or about that situation that He is trying to show and/ or teach us.

God can take us through any situation we find ourselves in and heal us while we are still in the mess, using His process if we allow Him to. But first we have to allow Jesus to renew our mind and this happens only when we set our mind on Him.

Philippians 4:8 - 4:9

8 Finally, brethren, whatsoever things are true, whatsoever things [are] honest, whatsoever things [are] just, whatsoever things [are] pure, whatsoever things [are] lovely, whatsoever things [are] of good report; if [there be] any virtue, and if [there be] any praise, think on these things. 9 Those things, which ye have both learned, and received, and heard, and seen in me, do: and the God of peace shall be with you.

Solution #1: Whenever we get into places where the negativity is so much that it is stifling, we need to go within. Go within and ask God to renew our mind. Think on all those things that God has done for us recently and dwell upon those things. Search our mind for positive thoughts. Don't allow the people or what's happening within the environment we find our self in to taint or askew our views. There are some environments that we simply do not need to be in (we know what they are). But for those that are unavoidable, find something positive to immerse your mind and energy field in. We don't have to go along with what everybody else is doing or thinking. See what you can learn from the situation to become a higher you.

2 Corinthians 10:4 - 10:5 4 *(For the weapons of our warfare [are] not carnal, but mighty through God to the pulling down of strong holds;) 5 Casting down imaginations, and every high thing that exalteth itself against the knowledge of God, and bringing into captivity every thought to the obedience of Christ;*

School: Our school system has grown more violent as each year passes. Our children may be going through rough periods in school; they are being killed; being bullied; treated unfairly by the teachers; they didn't make the team; they didn't win an election; they didn't get into a group and they feel rejected and/or dejected. Negative things are happening and negative thoughts may be plaguing our children. Help them by showing them that what the world says they are is not what God knows them to be.

Solution #3 - Create Family Routines: We can combat this negative environment by speaking positive words into our children and through prayer. We need to work into our children's lives the power of prayer and positive affirmations. We can take scriptures and powerful positive affirmations; write one or more on a piece of paper and place it in our child's pocket, notebook, lunchbox, or in their pencil box everyday and tell them to read it at some point in time during their day.

Before we send our children off into the lion's den, pray with them. Speak Jesus, His protection, His assistance, life, safety, success, confidence, humility, opportunities and open doors into our children before they leave out the house for school every morning. We can make it a habit for us and them. This can become a family routine that will last all parties a lifetime. We can set our mind on Jesus and through Jesus our minds and the minds of our children shall be renewed.

Group: Who We Spend Our Time With

The type of people we surround ourselves with will be reflected in our attitude, our thinking and how we treat people. This is true no matter what age we are. God showed me that we cannot choose to be around negative, back biting, and vindictive, gossiping, pessimistic, critical, judgmental, glass half empty, and downright ignorant people with limited mindsets and it not affect us. It's just not possible to be around people like that for any period of time having no effect on us. Remember they are of the world which is sinful and this is currently their natural state. This makes them more powerful than you think. They have the ability to suck you in before you know what happened.

He showed me that because we are spiritual and energy beings we draw from one another. But some at a faster rate than others. Did you ever notice how drained you felt after being around a particular person or group of people? This is because before we knew it, they sucked all the energy out of us and deposited it into themselves. They are parasites, well not them necessarily but the spirits that have attached themselves to and into the people we choose to spend our time with.

It is important to understand how the devil works. If we don't understand how he works we will remain in circumstances that are counterproductive to our walk with Jesus. The devil is a liar and he will prey on us under the guise of being our friend. But he has no good intention for us, only evil. The longer he can keep us around these negative and parasitic people, the stronger his hold on us becomes. To us these people are our friends or family and they love us. We like the same things and they listen to our problems and we listen to theirs.

That is the problem that we can't seem to see. The devil has us in a trap and we don't even know it. Sin has us in a trap and we don't even know it. Our familiar people could have us in a trap and we don't even know it. Misery loves company and if you are caught up in yours and other people's misery, you are not able to walk in the fullness of God. It is not until you come out of that negative mindset; come from around those negative people; and turn your eyes to Jesus that you will be able to truly see. Don't get caught in Satan's trap. Even though we love our family and friends we cannot allow them to keep us in bondage.

We must come to the decision that we don't want to stay in that negative headspace any longer. When we are stuck there we cannot fulfill God's promise in our lives. Negative thoughts only beget more negative thoughts. In that place of negativity and pessimism we block out the ability for joy, positive thoughts, positive happenings, or blessings that God consistently shower us with, to make its way through.

Everyone finds themselves around people like these over the course of their lives. However, no matter who they are to us, or how much we love them, we don't have to continue to partake in the nonsense. I know it's a strong word but it really is nonsense. It does not add value to our lives, it detracts from it. It does not propel us closer to our destiny, it sets us back. It does not allow us to walk in our purpose it puts us on a self centered path.

Solution - Renew Your Mind: God wants to provide more for us in every area of our life. However, in order for us to have what He wants for us, we have to get our mind right. When we allow God to show us who we are, we will no longer be attracted to people, places or things that detracts from us instead of adding.

In order to get our minds right we must first set our mind on God and allow Him to renew our mind. We do not have to sever relationships but we do have to limit our exposure to them. Make sure you are prayed up and anointed from head to toe before you willfully step into the fire. Ask God to bring you out safely and unscathed. Pray for your friends and loved ones that they too can come to know and accept Jesus as their Lord and personal Savior; and wake up and receive a renewed mind and transformed life.

Food: What We Deposit Into Our Spirit

He was not speaking of food to feed the physical body. He was speaking of the food we feed our spiritual bodies. It wasn't until God began to remove things from my life including my own desire for certain things that I began to understand this very principle. There are times my Daddy teaches me through experience and this principle was one of them. He removed people, traditional television and traditional radio. One by one God began removing things from my life.

First He removed people: There are times when people, no matter how much you love them are a distraction from what God needs you to see, know or receive. When you are trying desperately to walk with God and stay in a positive mindset the devil will use people to attack you and/or drag you down with their negative mentality. They want you to sit with them and gossip about other people; sit around while they talk themselves out of progress; sit around and talk about everything that is wrong with their lives; and bring drama and discord into your life. You can't go where God want to take you if you are stuck in darkness.

I emphatically will scream to anyone who will listen…"Don't Do It! Do not allow other people to drag you into sin. If it does not elevate you, don't do it. If it is not a positive word, thought or action don't speak it. You do not have to allow others to take you away from Gods light.

No more television: I lost complete interest in television. I don't know why I just did. Once I did that, it opened me up to pursue a path that led me closer to Jesus. I spent more and more time reading the bible. I began a meditation regimen. I was able to use music on Pandora to keep my mind in a state of worship. I began watching sermons on YouTube whereby I am able to watch and/or listen to them whenever I want to. I have endless energy to accomplish all the things I need to do daily. I am able to focus much more intently on any task I have to do. I spend as much time as possible depositing Godly words, teachings and uplifting music into myself because I found it allows me to remain in a positive and raised state. I am fed by these things. They add to me not detract from me. I've found that, because I don't watch the things I once did, I think at a different level than I use to.

What I choose to feed my spirit deposits into me, it feeds me. Regular television does not deposit anything positive into me. All it does is tell me that I'm not good enough. I don't have enough. I don't look the way I'm supposed to look. Everything is negative. Death, destruction, disruption, violence and craziness are few of the things that await us with regular television. There is no peace when we spend a lot of time watching television. I want what God has for me and I will not allow television to block me from my blessings. I may return to television, but it won't be the way it use to be.

No more radio: The only time I listen to traditional radio is when I'm in other people's car. I listen to a radio app that allows me to choose the type of music I want to hear. I don't have to hear cursing, sexually charged lyrics, lyrics about drinking and drugs, and lyrics about committing violent acts. Life itself can be stressful and negative all by itself. Why do I have to keep depositing negativity into myself? God taught me how to truly feed my spirit and I no longer go to the world to feed my spirit.

The world does not have what I need. This is what I found out once God removed it from my life. Isn't it funny how we don't know what were missing until you lose something and have to replace what we loss with something else. It is important that we remain vigilant to the things we allow into our lives and spirit. What we allow into ourselves will put and/or keep us in bondage or free and elevate us. We get to decide which one we will pursue. We have to get our mind right if we truly want to walk into the fullness of Christ?

Solution - Eat Right: Not only is it important to feed ourselves the right things every day but it is even more important to do so when we feel God trying to move us into another level in life. We will not be able to move ahead if you still think like you always did. If we are in a negative mindset we will not be able to accept what is on offer to us. Actually, when you are stuck in a negative mindset you won't even be able to see the opportunities being presented to you. When I eat I need it to fill me up. What is the point in being fed to only be hungrier than before I ate? Being fed by the world leaves me empty and I don't want to feel empty. Being fed by the word of God or music that's praising and worshiping Him, fills me up. So, God please!

It is very important that we do our part in developing a great relationship with God. He's always been the one lifting the heavy load, God's 99.99% to our .01% and as unfair as that may sound, our Daddy don't even mind. He yearns for us and it pains Him that we don't yearn for Him in return. How long will you live with a negative mindset?

How long will you allow opportunities to pass you by? How long will you wait to allow Jesus into your mind?

Will you dare to go against your current mindset and allow Jesus to renew it? *There are two things you can do to change the course of your life. You can accept Jesus Christ as your lord and personal savior and you can get the necessary assistance and tools to ensure you assist and not impede Him during your transformation.*

Asking for and accepting help from others is a choice, much like the choice we make to turn to God and accept the help and healing He offers to all who are alone and broken. The choice is yours to make but it's my prayer that you will make the choice that leads you to being transformed more and more into the image of Christ.

If you were fed by any of the messages I was given and would like to choose Jesus to be the ruler of your life, repeat this prayer.

Dear Heavenly Father, thank you for being a forgiving God. Thank you for giving your life up to save mine. Thank you for washing away my sins with the might of your blood. Father I ask you to come into my life and be my Lord and Savior. Humble me before you and ground me into dust and rebuild me into the person you want, need and know me to be to do all that you need me to do.

-Amen

IN MY DARKEST HOUR, HE APPEARED TO ME.

CHAPTER 23

IN MY DARKEST HOUR

CHAPTER 23

POEM: IN MY DARKEST HOUR

In my darkest hour,
He appeared to me.
With tears flowing down my cheeks I asked,
"What will become of me?"

As He drew closer and gazed upon me,
He smiled a beautiful smile.
He told me all will be well,
and I'd know in a short while.

"But please", I cried as He stood before me,
I cowered at His feet.
The pain is too great for me to bare,
let me explain–come have a seat.

I told Him all my problems and
showed Him all my scars.
He looked at me with sympathy,
and told me that I am not far.

It Was Good I Was Afflicted

I bowed my head before Him,
in acceptance of His word.
Although I did not understand and
it wasn't what I would have preferred.

As He turned away from me,
He laid His hand upon my head.
From that moment onward,
the old me was dead.

I looked the same on the outside and
the problems were still there,
But the peace He placed inside me,
no tribulations can ever compare.

~ Gail A Henry-Walker ~

I HOPE MY STORY AND MESSAGES RESONATED WITH YOU
TO CREATE POSITIVE FORWARD MOVING CHANGES OR
THOUGHTS IN YOUR OWN LIFE.

CHAPTER 24

FINAL THOUGHTS

CHAPTER 24

FINAL THOUGHTS

I greatly appreciate all of you that have allowed me into your space for a moment in time. I hope my story and messages resonated with you and encouraged you to create positive forward moving changes and thoughts in your own life.

I don't know why I have been chosen, I just know that I have been. My pain of yesteryear can become your triumph of today. My brokenness can become your portal to healing. Reach for something beyond yourself or another human being. I promise you they can't help you. Reach for Jesus. He will never leave you nor forsake you. He will give you peace and show you mercy and grace.

Allow Him to meet you and love you where you are right now. No matter where you are, if you still have breath and you call out to Him, He will come and get you. He wants to love you through your pain, mess, loneliness and brokenness. Call upon Him and let Him rescue you.

No matter the sin, if you call upon Him, He will come. Just scream out, "JESUS" and He will come. *38 For I am persuaded, that neither death, nor life, nor angels, nor principalities, nor powers, nor things present, nor things to come, 39 nor height, nor depth, nor any other creature, shall be able to separate us from the love of god, which is in Christ Jesus our lord. Romans 8:38-39 You don't need to get right first and then seek Him. He will take you just as you are.*

In the midst of your mess, you can call upon Him. Within the epicenter of your addictions, you can call upon Him. In the middle of your suicide decision you can call upon His name. When the world seems to be crashing all around you, you can call upon His name and He will come. Jesus is a God of hope, a God of healing, a God of redemption, a God of restoration, a God of resurrection, a God of love, a God of forgiveness, a God of grace and a God of transformation. Whatever you need Him to be for you, He is "THAT". God the Great "I AM" can and will become whatever He needs to become for you in any moment. Reach for Him and Him alone.

Romans 10:13 King James Version (KJV)13 For whosoever shall call upon the name of the Lord shall be saved.

NOTHING I'VE BEEN THROUGH WAS WASTED

LETS CONNECT!

LET'S CONNECT!

Http://Gailahenry.com

Http://www.itwasgoodiwasafflicted.com

Facebook@ GailAHenryASC

Twitter@ GailAHenryASC

Https://plus.google.com/u/0/+GailAHenryASC/posts

Instagram@ GailAHenryASC

Pinterest@GailAHenryASC/

AUTHOR – SPEAKER – COACH – ENTREPRENEUR

ABOUT THE AUTHOR

GAIL A HENRY-WALKER

ABOUT THE AUTHOR

Gail A Henry-Walker was born in Kingston, Jamaica to Rev. Val V Henry and Ruth M Henry. Ms. Henry-Walker is the CEO of multiple growing businesses under the LGT Media Group, LLC umbrella. LGT Media Group, LLC is a spirituality-focused media enterprise that brings God's word, His teachings, other positive messages, business opportunities, services and products to the people in an effort to change their lives. Gail strives to build enterprises that help to further God's kingdom and create financial freedom for her readers and customers.

Ms. Henry-Walker has been an Entrepreneur from a young age. She is also a Writer, Author, Life & Entrepreneurship Coach and Speaker. Ms. Henry-Walker has always believed that everyone has a purpose and in order for that purpose to be fulfilled, we will be required to clear out things within our self that don't serve us or our purpose.

As she went through her own transformation, she made it a point to pay close attention to the process and to the slightest changes that were taking place within her, even if she viewed them as insignificant. What she realized, was that nothing during her time of transformation was insignificant. All of it was relevant to who she was becoming and what God needed her to do. It was important that she paid attention and remained present through the experience. She wanted to participate in the process and put in the work.

Well, Gail did her work and God did and is still doing His (she's still a work in progress). She is grateful that God loved her enough to save, heal, deliver, restore and transform her. He took her from where she was and transported her into a new dimension with infinite possibilities. Ms. Henry-Walker bypasses any fears she may have, to step into the purpose that God created her to accomplish.

My purpose in life is to help girls and women who have been battered physically, mentally and spiritually by people and life, achieve a greater sense of peace, clarity, and spiritual awareness.

I'M BLESSED, I'M HEALED, I'M WHOLE

AND I'M CHANGED FOREVER